COMPREHENSIVE RESEARCH
AND STUDY GUIDE

Seamus
Heaney

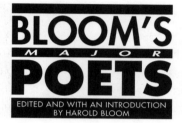

BLOOM'S
MAJOR
POETS

EDITED AND WITH AN INTRODUCTION
BY HAROLD BLOOM

CURRENTLY AVAILABLE

BLOOM'S MAJOR DRAMATISTS	BLOOM'S MAJOR NOVELISTS	BLOOM'S MAJOR POETS	BLOOM'S MAJOR SHORT STORY WRITERS
Aeschylus	Jane Austen	Maya Angelou	Jorge Luis Borges
Aristophanes	The Brontës	Elizabeth Bishop	Italo Calvino
Bertolt Brecht	Willa Cather	William Blake	Raymond Carver
Anton Chekhov	Stephen Crane	Gwendolyn Brooks	Anton Chekhov
Henrik Ibsen	Charles Dickens	Robert Browning	Joseph Conrad
Ben Johnson	William Faulkner	Geoffrey Chaucer	Stephen Crane
Christopher Marlowe	F. Scott Fitzgerald	Sameul Taylor Coleridge	William Faulkner
Arthur Miller	Nathaniel Hawthorne	Dante	F. Scott Fitzgerald
Eugene O'Neill	Ernest Hemingway	Emily Dickinson	Nathaniel Hawthorne
Shakespeare's Comedies	Henry James	John Donne	Ernest Hemingway
Shakespeare's Histories	James Joyce	H.D.	O. Henry
Shakespeare's Romances	D. H. Lawrence	T. S. Eliot	Shirley Jackson
Shakespeare's Tragedies	Toni Morrison	Robert Frost	Henry James
George Bernard Shaw	John Steinbeck	Seamus Heaney	James Joyce
Neil Simon	Stendhal	Homer	Franz Kafka
Oscar Wilde	Leo Tolstoy	Langston Hughes	D.H. Lawrence
Tennessee Williams	Mark Twain	John Keats	Jack London
August Wilson	Alice Walker	John Milton	Thomas Mann
	Edith Wharton	Sylvia Plath	Herman Melville
	Virginia Woolf	Edgar Allan Poe	Flannery O'Connor
		Poets of World War I	Edgar Allan Poe
		Shakespeare's Poems & Sonnets	Katherine Anne Porter
		Percy Shelley	J. D. Salinger
		Alfred, Lord Tennyson	John Steinbeck
		Walt Whitman	Mark Twain
		William Carlos Williams	John Updike
		William Wordsworth	Eudora Welty
		William Butler Yeats	

COMPREHENSIVE RESEARCH
AND STUDY GUIDE

Seamus Heaney

CHELSEA HOUSE
PUBLISHERS
A Haights Cross Communications ◢◤ Company
Philadelphia

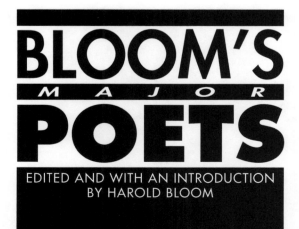

BLOOM'S *MAJOR* POETS

EDITED AND WITH AN INTRODUCTION
BY HAROLD BLOOM

© 2003 by Chelsea House Publishers, a subsidiary of
Haights Cross Communications.

Introduction © 2003 by Harold Bloom.

Printed and bound in the United States of America.

First Printing
1 3 5 7 9 8 6 4 2

Library of Congress Cataloging-in-Publication Data

Seamus Heaney / Harold Bloom, ed..
      p. cm. — (Bloom's major poets)
Includes bibliographical references and index.
    ISBN 0-7910-6816-1
    1. Heaney, Seamus—Criticism and interpretation. 2. Ireland—In
literature. I. Bloom, Harold. II. Series
    PR6058.E2 Z876 2002
    821'.914—dc21   2002005844

Chelsea House Publishers
1974 Sproul Road, Suite 400
Broomall, PA 19008-0914

The Chelsea House World Wide Web address is http://www.chelseahouse.com

Contributing Editor: Pamela Loos

Layout by EJB Publishing Services

CONTENTS

USER'S GUIDE

This volume is designed to present biographical, critical, and bibliographical information on the author and the author's best-known or most important short stories. Following Harold Bloom's editor's note and introduction is a concise biography of the author that discusses major life events and important literary accomplishments. A plot summary of each story follows, tracing significant themes, patterns, and motifs in the work. An annotated list of characters supplies brief information on the main characters in each story. As with any study guide, it is recommended that the reader read the story beforehand, and have a copy of the story being discussed available for quick reference.

A selection of critical extracts, derived from previously published material, follows each character list. In most cases, these extracts represent the best analysis available from a number of leading critics. Because these extracts are derived from previously published material, they will include the original notations and references when available. Each extract is cited, and readers are encouraged to check the original publication as they continue their research. A bibliography of the author's writings, a list of additional books and articles on the author and their work, and an index of themes and ideas conclude the volume.

ABOUT THE EDITOR

Harold Bloom is Sterling Professor of the Humanities at Yale University and Henry W. and Albert A. Berg Professor of English at the New York University Graduate School. He is the author of over 20 books, and the editor of more than 30 anthologies of literary criticism.

Professor Bloom's works include *Shelley's Mythmaking* (1959), *The Visionary Company* (1961), *Blake's Apocalypse* (1963), *Yeats* (1970), *A Map of Misreading* (1975), *Kabbalah and Criticism* (1975), *Agon: Toward a Theory of Revisionism* (1982), *The American Religion* (1992), *The Western Canon* (1994), and *Omens of Millennium: The Gnosis of Angels, Dreams, and Resurrection* (1996). *The Anxiety of Influence* (1973) sets forth Professor Bloom's provocative theory of the literary relationships between the great writers and their predecessors. His most recent books include *Shakespeare: The Invention of the Human*, a 1998 National Book Award finalist, *How to Read and Why* (2000), and *Stories and Poems for Extremely Intelligent Children of All Ages* (2001).

Professor Bloom earned his Ph.D. from Yale University in 1955 and has served on the Yale faculty since then. He is a 1985 MacArthur Foundation Award recipient and served as the Charles Eliot Norton Professor of Poetry at Harvard University in 1987–88. In 1999 he was awarded the prestigious American Academy of Arts and Letters Gold Medal for Criticism. Professor Bloom is the editor of several other Chelsea House series in literary criticism, including BLOOM'S MAJOR SHORT STORY WRITERS, BLOOM'S MAJOR NOVELISTS, BLOOM'S MAJOR DRAMATISTS, MODERN CRITICAL INTERPRETATIONS, MODERN CRITICAL VIEWS, and BLOOM'S BIOCRITIQUES.

EDITOR'S NOTE

My Introduction centers upon Heaney's *North* and *Field Work*, with observations upon "North," "Singing School," "Glanmore Sonnets," and "The Harvest Bow," among others.

I cite here only a handful of the many "Critical Views" excerpted in this volume. Henry Hart reads "North" as undoing heroic myth, while Eammon Hughes finds in "Singing School" Heaney's agon with tradition.

Michael Parker traces the strands that come together in "Glanmore Sonnets," after which Henry Hart returns to contrast the depictions of the father-son relationship in "The Harvest Bow" and in earlier poems.

"Ugolino" is found by Tony Curtis to be a reflection of Irish history, while "Station Island" is studied by Darcy O'Brien in particular regard to the poem's dark conclusion.

Helen Vendler, the most distinguished of Heaney's critics, praises the maturing vision of "The Haw Lantern," which gives us the poet at his strongest.

Harold Bloom

I hear behind the poems of *North* the middle Yeats of *The Green Helmet* and of *Responsibilities*, a hearing reinforced by *Field Work*. This is the Yeats of a vision counting still its human cost, and so not yet abandoned to daemonic presences and intensities:

> I passed through the eye of the quern,
>
> Grist to an ancient mill,
> And in my mind's eye saw
> A world-tree of balanced stones,
> Querns piled like vertebrae,
> The marrow crushed to grounds.

This is Heaney's "Belderg" from *North*, but I do not think Yeats would have disowned it. The enduring poems in *North* include the majestic title-piece, as well as "Funeral Rites," "Kinship," "Whatever You Say, Say Nothing," and, best of all, the sequence of poetic incarnations with the Yeatsian title, "Singing School." The poem "North" gave and still gives Heaney his poetics, as a mythic voice proclaims what must be this new poet's relation to the Irish past:

> It said, "Lie down
> in the word-hoard, burrow
> the coil and gleam
> of your furrowed brain.
>
> Compose in darkness.
> Expect aurora borealis
> in the long foray
> but no cascade of light.
>
> Keep your eye clear
> as the bleb of the icicle,
> trust the feel of what nubbed treasure
> your hands have known."

The reader of *Field Work* comes to realize that Heaney's eye is as clear, through discipline, as the air bubbles in an icicle, as clear, say, as the American eye of the late Elizabeth Bishop. "Funeral Rites" inaugurates what seems doomed to be Heaney's central mode, whether he finally chooses Dublin or Belfast. "Kinship," a more difficult sequence, salutes the bog country as the "outback of my mind" and then flows into a grander trope:

> This is the vowel of earth
> dreaming its root
> in flowers and snow,
>
> mutation of weathers
> and seasons,
> a windfall composing
> the floor it rots into.
>
> I grew out of all this
> like a weeping willow
> inclined to
> the appetites of gravity.

Such inevitability of utterance would be more than enough if it were merely personal; it would suffice. Its grandeur is augmented in the last section of "Kinship" when Heaney acquires the authentic authority of becoming the voice of his people:

> Come back to this
> 'island of the ocean'
> where nothing will suffice.
> Read the inhumed faces
>
> of casualty and victim;
> report us fairly,
> how we slaughter
> for the common good
>
> and shave the heads
> of the notorious,
> how the goddess swallows
> our love and terror.

The problem for Heaney as a poet henceforward is how not to drown in this blood-dimmed tide. His great precedent is the Yeats of "Meditations in Time of Civil War" and "Nineteen Hundred and Nineteen," and it cannot be said in *North* that this precedent is met, even in "Whatever You Say, Say Nothing," where the exuberance of the language achieves a genuine phantasmagoria. But "Singing

School," with its queerly appropriate mix of Wordsworth and Yeats, does even better, ending poem and book with a finely rueful self-accepting portrait of the poet, still waiting for the word that is his alone:

> I am neither internee nor informer;
> And inner émigré, grown long-haired
> And thoughtful; a wood-kerne
>
> Escaped from the massacre,
> Taking protective colouring
> From bole and bark, feeling
> Every wind that blows;
>
> Who, blowing up these sparks
> For their meagre heat, have missed
> The once-in-a-lifetime portent,
> The comet's pulsing rose.

That is true eloquence, but fortunately not the whole truth, as *Field Work* richly shows. Heaney is the poet of the vowel of earth and not of any portentous comet. In *Field Work*, he has gone south, away from Belfast violence. No poem in *Field Work* is without its clear distinction, but I exercise here the critic's privilege of discussing those poems that move me most: "Casualty," "The Badgers," "The Singer's House," the lovely sequence of ten "Glanmore Sonnets," "The Harvest Bow" (Heaney's masterpiece so far), and the beautiful elegy "In Memoriam Francis Ledwidge," for the Irish poet killed on the Western Front in 1917. All of these lyrics and meditations practice a rich negation, an art of excluded meanings, vowels of earth almost lost between guttural consonants of history. Heaney's Irish sibyl warns him that "The ground we kept our ear to for so long / Is flayed or calloused." The muted elegy "Casualty," which cunningly blends the modes of Yeats's "The Fisherman" and "Easter 1916," concludes in a funeral march giving us the sea's version of Heaney's vowel of earth:

> They move in equal pace
> With the habitual
> Slow consolation
> of dawdling engine,
> The line lifted, hand

Over fist, cold sunshine
On the water, the land
Banked under fog: that morning
I was taken in his boat,
The screw purling, turning
Indolent fathoms of white,
I tasted freedom with him.
To get out early, haul
Steadily off the bottom,
Dispraise the catch, and smile
As you find a rhythm
Working you, slow mile by mile,
Into your proper haunt
Somewhere, well out, beyond . .

Even as the slain fisherman's transcendence fuses with Heaney's catch of a poem to send the poet also "beyond," so Heaney has revised Yeats's ambition by having written an elegy as passionate as the perpetual night of the Troubles. Even stronger is "The Badger," an oblique poem of deepest self-questioning, in which the elegiac strain is evaded and all simple meanings are thwarted. Sensing "some soft returning," whether of the murdered dead or of the badgers, Heaney places upon his reader the burden of difficult interpretation:

Visitations are taken for signs.
At a second house I listened
for duntings under the laurels
and heard intimations whispered
about being vaguely honoured.

The first line of this passage does not reach back to Lancelot Andrewes through Eliot's "Gerontion" but rather itself boldly revises John 4:48, "Except ye see signs and wonders, ye will not believe" and perhaps even Matthew 12:38-39. "An evil and adulterous generation seeketh after a sign." The duntings are at once the dull sounds of badgers and, more crucially, the Wordsworthian "low breathings" of *The Prelude* I, 323. Though an external haunting, testifying to the laurels of poetic election "vaguely honoured," they are also Heaney's hard-drawn breaths, in this text and out of it, in a murderous Northern Ireland. Heaney, once so ruggedly simplistic in his only apparent stance, has entered upon the agonistic way of a stronger poetry, necessarily denser, more allusive, and persuasively difficult.

I read this entrance as the triumph of "The Singer's House," a poem I will forbear quoting entire, though I badly want to, and give only the superb three stanzas of the conclusion, where Heaney laments the loss of everything in his land that should be "crystal," and discovers an inevitable image for his audacious and determined art that would reverse lament and loss:

> People here used to believe
> that drowned souls lived in the seals.
> At the spring tides they might change shape.
> They loved music and swam in for a singer
>
> who might stand at the end of summer
> in the mouth of a whitewashed turf-shed,
> his shoulder to the jamb, his song
> a rowboat far out in evening.
>
> When I came here first you were always singing,
> a hint of the clip of the pick
> in you winnowing climb and attack.
> Raise it again, man. We still believe what we hear.

The verve of that final line is a tonic even for an American reader like myself, cut off from everything local that inspires and appalls Heaney. Closer to ordinary evenings in New Haven are the universal concerns that rise out of the local in the distinguished "Glanmore Sonnets" that open, again, with Heaney's central trope: "Vowels ploughed into other: opened ground." Confronting an image of the good life as field work, with art redeemed from violence and so "a paradigm" of new-ploughed earth, Heaney finds even in the first sonnet that his ghosts come striding back. Against the ghosts he seeks to set his own story as a poet who could heed Moneta's admonition to Keats, or Nietzsche's to all of us: "Think of the earth."

> Then I landed in the hedge-school of Glanmore
> And from the backs of ditches hoped to raise
> A voice caught back off slug-horn and slow chanter
> That might continue, hold, dispel, appease:
> Vowels ploughed into other: opened ground,
> Each verse returning like the plough turned round.

Yet the ninth sonnet is driven to ask with true desperation: "What is my apology for poetry?" and the superb tenth sonnet ends the sequence overtly echoing Wyatt's most passionate moment, while more darkly and repressively alluding to the Yeatsian insight of the perpetual virginity of the soul: "the lovely and painful / Covenants of flesh; our separateness." More hopeful, but with a qualified hope, is the perfect lyric "The Harvest Bow," which I quote in its entirety:

> As you plaited the harvest bow
> You implicated the mellowed silence in you
> In wheat that does not rust
> But brightens as it tightens twist by twist
> Into a knowable corona,
> A throwaway love-knot of straw.
>
> Hands that aged round ashplants and cane sticks
> And lapped the spurs on a lifetime of games cocks
> Harked to their gift and worked with fine intent
> Until your fingers moved somnambulant:
> I tell and finger it like braille,
> Gleaning the unsaid off the palpable,
>
> And if I spy into its golden loops
> I see us walk between the railway slopes
> Into an evening of long grass and midges,
> Blue smoke straight up, old beds and ploughs in hedges,
> An auction notice on a outhouse wall—
> You with a harvest bow in your lapel,
>
> Me with the fishing rod, already homesick
> For the big lift of evenings, as your stick
> Whacking the tips off weeds and bushes
> Beats out of time, and beats, but flushes
> Nothing: that original townland
> Still tongue-tied in the straw by your hand.
>
> *The end of art is peace*
> Could be the motto of this frail device
> That I have pinned up on our deal dresser—
> Like a drawn snare
> Slipped lately by the spirit of the corn
> Yet burnished by its passage, and still warm.

Heaney could not have found a more wistful, Clare-like emblem than the love knot of straw for this precariously beautiful poem, or a sadder, gentler motto than: *"The end of art is peace."* Certainly the oversong of the poem, its stance as love-lyric, seems to sing against Yeats's Paterian ringers in the tower, who have appointed for the hymeneal of the soul a passing bell. But the end of married love may be peace; the end of art is agonistic, against time's "it was," and so against anterior art.

The hands which plait the harvest bow are masculine and hardened, but delicate in the office of marriage, which brings in harvest. Implicated in the making is the knowable corona of mellowed silence, not the unreliable knowledge of poetry; and Heaney as poet must both love and stand back and away from this wisdom, paternal and maternal. The fingers which follow a human tradition can move as if moving in sleep – "asleep in its own life," as Stevens said of the child. But Heaney must "tell and finger it like braille," for that is the poet's field of work: "Gleaning the unsaid off the palpable," the slender pickings after the granary is full.

Though his vision, *through her emblem*, in the third stanza approximates a true peace, it breaks into something both richer and more forlorn in what comes after. The young Yeats sang of "The Happy Townland," where "Boughs have their fruit and blossom / At all times of the year" and "all that are killed in battle / Awaken to life again." Heaney, leaving youth, hears in recollections of innocent venery a music that "Beats out of time, and beats, but flushes / Nothing." There is nothing for it to start up since the happy or original townland belongs only to those "still tongue-tied" in the frail device of the harvest bow. Heaney's genius is never surer than in his all-but-undoing of this emblem in his final trope, where the love knot becomes a drawn snare recently evaded by a corn-king, an evasion that itself both burnishes and animates the knowable corona of achieved marriage. Obliquely but firmly, the struggle of poetry displaces the lover's stance, and the undersong finds a triumph in the poem's closure.

I verge upon saying that Heaney approaches the cunning stance of the strong poet, evasion, for which I cite not its American theorists and bards, from Emerson through Whitman and Dickinson to Frost and Stevens but the central British master of the mode:

> Know ye not then the Riddling of the Bards?
> Confusion, and illusion, and relation,
> Elusion, and occasion, and evasion?

That is Tennyson's Seer, not Emerson's Merlin, and must become Heaney's poetic, if like Yeats he is to transcend the vowel of earth. It will be a painful transition for a poet whose heart is with the visionary naturalism of Wordsworth and Keats and Clare (and Kavanagh, Montague, R. S. Thomas) rather than with a vision fighting free of earth. But there are signs in *Field Work* that the transition is under way. Heaney ends the book with a grim rendition of Dante's Ugolino, too relevant to the Irish moment, and with his not altogether successful title poem which invokes the Gnostic doubloon of Melville's Ahab. I end here by reading in the noble quatrains of Heaney's "In Memoriam Francis Ledwidge" a powerful evasion of a fate that this poet will never accept as his own:

> In you, our dead enigma, all the strains
> Criss-cross in useless equilibrium
> And as the wind tunes through this vigilant bronze
> I hear again the sure confusing drum
>
> You followed from Boyne water to the Balkans
> But miss the twilit note your flute should sound.
> You were not keyed or pitched like these true-blue ones
> Though all of you consort now underground.

Not my way to go, as Heaney tells us, for he is keyed and pitched unlike any other significant poet now at work in the language, anywhere. The strains criss-cross in him so useful an equilibrium that all critics and lovers of poetry must wish him every cunning for survival. To this critic, on the other side of the Atlantic, Heaney is joined now with Geoffrey Hill as a poet so severe and urgent that he compels the same attention as his strongest American contemporaries, and indeed as only the very strongest among them.

Seamus Heaney

"The most important Irish poet since Yeats"—so has Seamus Heaney been described by the American poet Robert Lowell, who later in his life would become friends with Heaney. The intensity of the Irish experience is portrayed in much of the work of Heaney, who was born on April 13, 1939 on a family farm in Northern Ireland, about thirty miles northwest of Belfast. He was the first child of Margaret and Patrick Heaney, whose family would eventually grow to include nine children. This Catholic family was part of the majority that lived in the local area in relative harmony with their Protestant neighbors, yet at an early age Heaney felt the tension between the groups and within himself because of their divergent views on politics and religion, and, important for a future poet, their different languages and literary traditions.

By 1951 he was boarding at St. Columb's College in Londonderry on a scholarship. Here he had a very good English teacher and began to love reading, absorbing diverse material, from comic books to great literature. From 1957 until 1961 he studied at Queen's University in Belfast. It was here that he was impressed by the work of Robert Frost and Ted Hughes and so started writing his own poetry, some of which was published in the school's literary magazine. He received a degree in English language and literature with first-class honors and moved on to post-graduate work and attaining a teacher's certificate at St. Joseph's College of Education in Belfast. While studying there from 1961 to 1962, he gained a more extensive understanding of English literature and made his first true venture into studying Irish poetry. Also during this year, he joined a literary group lead by the English writer Philip Hobsbaum, who encouraged and helped Heaney and the other young writers in their efforts. The group provided a much-needed literary oasis for Heaney through 1966, and it was during this time that some of his poems were first published outside the university setting.

From 1962 to 1963 he taught at St. Thomas's Secondary School in Belfast, and from 1963 through 1966 he was lecturer in English at St. Joseph's College. He also began to write reviews and other pieces for the *New Statesman* and other periodicals. Personally and professionally this proved quite a time of accomplishment for the still-young Heaney. In 1965 his *Eleven Poems* was published as a pamphlet, and he married Marie Devlin that same year in August. In May 1966, his first book of poems, *Death of a Naturalist,* was published, and in July his son Michael was born. While this first poetry collection was generally well-received, by some it has been seen as uneven although still presenting a true and direct view of youth's response to the natural rural world. In that same year, Heaney was appointed lecturer in modern English literature at Queen's University and started work with the BBC radio and television as a contributor to their educational broadcasts.

Heaney's second son, Christopher, was born in February 1968, and by 1969 his second collection of poems was published, *Door into the Dark,* which also contained striking description of the physical world yet went beyond this to study myth, the unconscious, and the supernatural. In general, it gained a good critical response.

Political violence reached an intensity in Northern Ireland in 1969, and so Heaney and his family welcomed a respite in California, where Heaney became guest lecturer for the 1970-71 academic year at the University of California at Berkeley. The experience proved valuable in a number of ways. Protests at Berkeley over the Vietnam War and social injustice reminded Heaney of the unrest in his own country and showed him that poets could be a driving political force at such times. Additionally, Heaney was exposed to more American poetry and later reported that encountering this, and especially the work of William Carlos Williams, would inspire him to give his own writing a more relaxed structure.

In 1972 the Heaney's were offered a longer retreat by a friend of theirs who had a country cottage to rent in Glanmore, in the south of Ireland. Viewing it as a superb opportunity to dedicate himself to his writing, Heaney quit his post at Queen's University and the family packed their belongings. His collection *Wintering Out* (1972) was published shortly after this and received an ambivalent response. Its poems moved outside the personal and natural to the broader public sphere, yet some critics said about this, as they have about other of his work, that it showed a too-limited range.

At Glanmore in 1973, Heaney's third child, Catherine Ann, was born, and as the family continued their life of relative seclusion Heaney felt his marriage, family relationships, and writing blossom. While the family lived for a few years at the cottage, during this time Heaney also traveled to give poetry readings in England and the United States, edited two poetry anthologies and wrote numerous essays. Also, he began work on a translation of a Middle Irish romance that would be published as *Sweeney Astray* later in 1984. By 1975 his collection *North* appeared, with its first part emphasizing the mythic and the second focusing on the political Northern Ireland and the role of the poet. Critics in Belfast were not so impressed, but elsewhere the response was mostly positive.

In 1975 Heaney became head of the English department at Caryfort College, a teacher-training school in Dublin. Refreshed from country living but feeling he had secluded his family long enough, Heaney moved them to Dublin. His collection *Field Work* was published in 1979 and received generally strong reviews. In 1980, two books appeared—*Selected Poems 1965-1975,* and *Preoccupations: Selected Prose*, which contains essays on poets as well as frank discussion of his own poetic growth.

Continuing to stay connected with the United States through poetry readings, in 1982 Heaney accepted a five-year assignment to teach each spring semester at Harvard University in Massachusetts; this would grow into a permanent arrangement, and in 1984 he was named Boylston Professor of Rhetoric and Oratory. In 1984 his book *Station Island* was published and, for the most part, well-received. In 1987 his book *The Haw Lantern* was published. In 1989, Heaney was also named Professor of Poetry at Oxford University in England for a five-year period, requiring him to deliver three public lectures each year. In 1990 *New and Selected Poems, 1969-1987* was published, followed shortly thereafter in 1991 by *Seeing Things: Poems*. Additional publications include *The Midnight Verdict* (1993), *The Spirit Level* (1996), *Opened Ground: Selected Poems, 1966-1996* (1998) and his best-selling translation of *Beowulf,* which was published in 2000. In 1995 Heaney was awarded the Nobel Prize, and the committee extolled him for his "works of lyrical beauty and ethical depth, which exalt everyday miracles and the living past."

CRITICAL ANALYSIS OF

"North"

"North" was published in 1975 in a collection of poetry with the same name. The volume garnered both positive and negative responses, due in part to aroused sensitivities as a result of pervasive violence in Northern Ireland that had intensified since 1969. Indeed, Heaney's work had shifted in focus in this book. Now it attempted to take his personal past as well as his country's and provide perspective on its current state, one that seemed at times in danger of being radically oversimplified. In contrast, most of Heaney's earlier work had been pastoral and personal.

The poem "North" starts with a somewhat contemplative tone and is therefore fittingly slow in its sound. The first line—"I returned to a long strand,"—while only six syllables, has three that slow the reader with their drawn-out sounds ("turned," "long," "strand"). The second line follows a similar arrangement—short, with mostly lengthy-sounding syllables. The poem takes place somewhere that the narrator has been before, so we assume he has some comfort here. By the last two lines, though, there is a shift away from comfort. This place is not exactly as he had expected; he had anticipated finding something more here. For the Atlantic is described as having "*only* (emphasis added) the secular powers," as if the narrator thought either this ocean would have more power or that something other than the ocean would be here and that that would have more than only secular powers. Perhaps, also, since as the poem progresses we realize it is about violence, the secular nature of the sea is actually an escape from the religious confrontations in Heaney's Ireland. In any case, at this point in the poem there also is no more relatively mellow, contemplative tone, for the Atlantic, we are told, is "thundering," an ominously ringing word.

The narrator is looking toward Iceland and Greenland, described as "unmagical" and "pathetic." We see his disgust with violent aggressors and his distate for the victimized "pathetic colonies" as well. Both sides are seen as wrong, and both can evoke sympathy also. (In his poetry, Heaney refuses to go with the seemingly natural choice of aligning himself with those of his own background. He forces himself to question his instinctive reactions that are based on his Catholic nationalism.) Then "suddenly" the narrator sees the adversaries differently. The word "suddenly" ends the last line of the second stanza, and, indeed, we race through the next two stanzas because the lines are all preliminary description leading to the verb. There is another surprise between the second and third stanzas, for while previously these lands the narrator is viewing were seen negatively, now in the beginning of the third stanza, they are described as home to "fabulous raiders."

As the poem continues, though, "fabulous" will be seen as an adjective that is used facetiously. For Iceland's Norsemen, while good fighters, had suffered. That suffering took place not only in other territories, but for years in their own land, where there was chronic infighting, savage murders, and political chaos, ultimately resulting in 1262 in the land losing its independence. We already see in the second and third stanzas that there is little that is "fabulous" about warriors' death. While the Norsemen did, historically, invade other lands, including Ireland, and while museums show their might, in the poem the men are described as "lying in Orkney and Dublin," (Orkney is a group of islands off of Scotland that constitutes one of its counties) presumably dead, with even their swords "rusting" in uselessness. Even more grotesque and pitiful is the description of them "hacked and glinting / in the gravel of thawed streams," maimed and not even buried.

By the fifth stanza, the dead have voices. Even their ship has now come to life; "buoyant with hindsight" it has a voice and speaks to the narrator:

> Thor's hammer swung
> to geography and trade,
> thick-witted couplings and revenges,
>
> the hatreds and behind-backs
> of the althing, lies and women,
> exhaustions nominated peace,
> memory incubating the spilled blood.

We see what lies at the base of the Norse motivation in this description. Thor, the god of thunder in Norse mythology, swings his hammer, apparently the same tool that must have had such power it "hammered" the curve of the land that was described in the first stanza. This hammer operates first, we are told, on "geography and trade," subdued language for what history actually showed to be not just heroic exploration of unknown lands but the conquering of these lands and stealing of their goods. But after this description, the speaking ship is frank, admitting the hatred and evil consuming its people. The only times of peace, it said, was when the people reached exhaustion, and, horrifically, even during these times they were only lying in wait, "incubating" the violence for the next round. This is an appropriate description, Heaney seems to be saying, of the violence in Northern Ireland involving his own people as well.

From the eighth stanza through the poem's end, the ship directly tells the narrator, who we recognize also as the poet, what he is to do. The ship's voice is the only one here. "'Lie down / in the word-hoard," he tells the poet, meaning the poet must take up the task of his profession, getting in touch with the right words. To do this he is to "burrow" the negativity, the history, the pain, and all their accoutrements that are residing in his "furrowed brain," so that he can be in darkness, starting fresh from the black, tapping into the repository that resides within himself and needs a clear voice. The task is not easy and will take time, but it is his responsibility. He should anticipate some moments of light / insight, but no great assistance: "Expect aurora borealis / in the long foray / but no cascade of light."

But the last stanza explains why the poet will not need help. He must keep himself unencumbered like "the bleb of the icicle," which is the drip that comes from the icicle's tip as well as the air bubble inside. This is fitting, one critic has explained, for the fact that it is both clear but distorting around its curved edges, and applicable to Heaney's own situation of being suspended between the colder Northern Ireland and the warmer south. If the poet can keep himself focused and clear, he will see that all he needs is inside himself. He can trust his instinct, "the feel of what nubbed treasure / your hands have known."

In light of Heaney's heritage and previous work, it is not surprising that in the last three stanzas where the ship speaks that he uses natural imagery of the land, darkness, sky, ice. It marks his need to look back to what existed before man and his hatred, at what was pure, and at what was then used by his people and eventually his father to make a life. In previous pieces, he also compares a poet's life to that of a ploughman, digging and uncovering, each with the appropriate instruments.

CRITICAL VIEWS ON

"North"

P.R. KING ON NATURE AS SALVE

[P.R. King has been Lecturer in Education at Loughborough University, Leicestershire, England. In the following extract he explains Heaney's belief that to remove Ireland's woes, one must retreat to the land and the ocean, for these existed before the religious animosity that created Ireland's long-standing grief.]

It is *North* that really begins to provide the sense of that centre to his identity around which Heaney seems to have been circling. In it he pursues the honing of his style begun in the previous volume and in the clean, clear sweep of these poems the continuities and coherences really begin to be gathered up.

The title poem presents the poet looking out over the Atlantic from 'a long strand, / the hammered shod of a bay' from where he hears 'the secular / powers' of the sea and can look north towards Iceland. Standing there he is well placed geographically and metaphorically to look into the cold heart of northern Europe. His mind fills with the 'violence and epiphany' of the Norsemen who linked Iceland, Greenland, Scandinavia and Ireland, and he remembers the tombs, monuments and relics of that warrior race scattered between Orkney and Dublin in museums and in

> . . . the solid
> belly of stone ships,
> those hacked and glinting
> in the gravel of thawed streams.

These memories crowd together and link war, travel and trade, 'thick-witted couplings and revenges', whose memory incubates spilled blood. The past is redolent with the same violent revenges as the present. But to the poet these northern histories and legends, landscapes and hatreds, travels and tongues, are all contained in that 'long strand' which is the essence of Ireland. The Atlantic that bore the longboats with their 'swimming tongue . . . buoyant with hindsight' is to the poet a source of 'secular powers' which can replace the religious bigotry that is at root of the long history of violence because that ocean *precedes* all religious differences. The land was there before man. The poem ends with the 'longship's swimming tongue' pronouncing invocation and command:

> 'Lie down
>
> in the word-hoard, burrow
> the coil and gleam
> of your furrowed brain.
>
> Compose in darkness.
> Expect aurora borealis
> in the long foray
> but no cascade of light.
>
> Keep your eye clear
> at the bleb of the icicle,
> trust the feel of what nubbed treasure
> your hands have known.'

The poet is to dig down into the past, beneath even the violent history, to close with the earth and sea that clutches and drowns remnants of the past (wrecks, flints in pebbles, bodies preserved in the peatbogs—each of which have poems to themselves elsewhere in the latest volumes). He must cling to what he already knows, to what the land preserves; he is to search out the 'word-hoard' of this ancient language.

The form of this poem is sparse and ribbed compared with the heavier, more opulent language of the earliest poems. The lean line and free rhythm (a basic two-/three-stress system) are given more power by the diction. From the metaphor of the rocky shore ('hammered shod of a bay') to the cool, bright light of the aurora borealis, we are presented with a pattern of imagery that suggests cold, hard edges and which captures the landscape and its climate, the nature of the Norse raiders and the poet's determination.

The 'word-hoard' is explicitly stated in this poem, and it begins to call up threads from other poems, such as 'Anahorish', which have also used the language metaphor to connect place and past with the poet's task. This metaphor becomes dominant as a symbol over this whole volume. The poet speaks, but the land, its history, objects and people speak through him in each poem.

—P.R. King, *Nine Contemporary Poets*, (London and New York: Methuen & Co., 1979): pp. 214-16.

HENRY HART ON HEANEY'S DISMANTLING OF HEROIC MYTHS

[Henry Hart teaches at the College of William and Mary. He is the author of books of poems as well as books on other writers, including *James Dickey: The Life & Lies of a Poet*. Here he reveals how Heaney uses the romanticized myths of other cultures to make blatant the senselessness of Ireland's own continuing violence.]

The poet's actual return to a particular beach on the Atlantic coast typifies ["North's] many other returns. The voices of dead northerners, for example, return from the sea, "lifted again / in violence and epiphany," just as St. John's apocalyptic sea returns the dead to be judged. Heaney cancels the biblical supposition of a timeless new heaven and new earth by reaffirming the old world and old hell of history. History rumbles on to the cacophonous din of Thor's hammer blows and toward a last judgment that is pagan and secular. Thor, rather than Christ, judges the dead for their deeds. Heaney may recall a similar iconoclastic vision at the end of Sylvia Plath's "Blackberrying," where she looks "out on nothing, nothing but a great space" of ocean waves "like silversmiths / Beating and beating at an intractable metal," Heaney declares,

> I returned to a long strand,
> the hammered shod of a bay,
> and found only the secular
> powers of the Atlantic thundering.

If Auden succumbed to the pagan 'magic' of Iceland and its sagas, Heaney alludes to the sagas only to dismiss their deceptive romanticism. His apocalypse strives to purge the 'heroic' dross from the hard historical facts.

> I faced the unmagical
> invitations of Iceland,
> the pathetic colonies
> of Greenland, and suddenly

27

<blockquote>
those fabulous raiders,
those lying in Orkney and Dublin.
</blockquote>

Half-enchanted by the heroic dead, he delineates a *via negativa* in which their "ocean-deafened," Sirenlike voices fade away so that their real voices can be heard. Their "warning" is the "epiphany" that reveals the mystique that later generations have bestowed upon them and exposes their rapacious, bloodthirsty lives for what they were. *Njal's Saga*, which Heaney refers to in "Funeral Rites" and no doubt is remembering here, as one writer put it, recounts "the years of savage internal strife, murderous intrigues, and ruthless self-seeking power-politics that led, in 1262, to the loss of the independence that her [Iceland's] pioneers had created" (Magnusson and Palsson 1960, 10). From the *Saga*'s anonymous author, writing around 1280 of the chronic feuding among Iceland's Norsemen, Heaney garners sobering lessons for his own bellicose culture seven hundred years later.

Bearing in mind the *Saga*'s preoccupation with marriages that go wrong (between Unn and Hrut, Thorvald and Hallgerd, Gunnar and Hallgerd, to name a few), murders that burgeon from broken alliances, and grimly comic attempts to appease them at the *althing* (the judicial and legislative parliament of the Icelanders), and the ultimate entropy of the principal blood feud between Kari and Flosi (who killed Njal), Heaney renounces its epic pretentions. 'Heroic' journeys, like those by the Vikings and Norsemen, or those by the English and Scots in their conquest of Ireland, for Heaney are essentially brutal ventures initiated for territorial and economic gain. Heaney returns to myths and histories of primitive cultures that resemble his, stripping the old gods of their grandiose cloaks and implicating them in the worldly affairs from which they arose. He could be speaking of either ancient Icelanders or modern Irelanders when he observes,

<blockquote>
Thor's hammer swung
to geography and trade,
thick-witted couplings and revenges,
</blockquote>

<blockquote>
the hatreds and behindbacks
of the althing, lies and women,
exhaustions nominated peace,
memory incubating the spilled blood.
</blockquote>

If Heaney is thinking of Bernadette Devlin and other women in the civil rights battles of the late sixties and early seventies, they are surely tame compared to their Icelandic precursors like Hallgerd, who ordered her first husband's head split open with an axe, mustered death squads to pillage and murder her foes, and colluded with Gunnar's attackers in his fatal last stand.

—Henry Hart, Seamus Heaney: *Poet of Contrary Progressions*, (Syracuse: Syracuse University Press, 1992): pp. 79-81.

RAND BRANDES ON HEANEY'S CONNECTIONS BETWEEN POET AND PLOUGHMAN

[Rand Brandes teaches English at Lenoir Rhyne College in North Carolina. He is the co-editor of *Seamus Heaney: A Reference Guide*. Here he remarks on Heaney's imagery that presents the similarities of working with pen, plough, spade and many other instruments of labor.]

Since his first acclaimed poem, "Digging," Seamus Heaney has considered writing as work. The pen that replaces the spade becomes the poet's tool. The limpid analogy, which reduces "physical labor to a metaphor for cultural labor," is one source of the poem's enchantment. The poet as digger obviously foreshadows the poet as archaeologist. In between these two metapoetic tropes Heaney also uses the diviner, the thatcher, and the smith (among other) figures as analogues for the poet. Each figure's trade requires crafts and techniques that appear transferable to the work of the poet. The digger, diviner, and archaeologist are representative of a writing process in which the object of their search precedes them in both time and space. They *discover* their desired artifact, and in this way the writing process itself becomes its own end. The smith and thatcher, in contrast, produce their artifacts. The poem becomes a product and to a certain extent relinquishes its claims of originality. The scribe is an amalgamation of the poet as discoverer and the poet as producer. (. . .)

In *North* the allusions to the act of writing, letters, and the possible etymological fecundity of language take a more primitive orientation. The scribe's interest in writing focuses on the ancient and prehistoric inscriptions (lost languages and opaque ideograms) that are written into the world and transcribed in the poem. Even though the poet's language in *North* echoes the early word poems, as in "*moss*" and "*bawn*" from Belderg (*N* 14), the scribal tropes include cave drawings, scrimshaw, Braille, hieroglyphics, scribblings, and longhands.

The more literary terms, such as, "dictions," "latins," and "consonants" (*N* 28), join with the other scribal allusions to produce a self-reflexive metalinguistic substratum in *North*. In "Belderg," for example, the "first plough-marks, / the stone-age fields, the tomb" (13) provide prehistoric reference points for the central scribal trope in the poem "North":

> It said, "Lie down
> in the word-hoard, burrow
> the coil and gleam
> of your furrowed brain.["]
> (20)

Heaney's "word-hoard"—which recalls David Jones's "word-hoard"—is imagistically connected to the "first plough-marks" of "Belderg." The prehistoric ploughed furrow looks to the origins of poetry as Heaney sees them: "The poet as ploughman, if you like, and the suggestive etymology of the word 'verse.' . . . 'Verse' comes from the Latin *versus* which could mean a line of poetry but could also mean the turn that a ploughman made at the head of the field as he finished one furrow and faced back into another" (*Pr* 65). The ploughed furrow links not only the poet and the ploughman but also the poet and the scribe. A riddle written by a medieval scribe makes this connection clear:

> An iron point
> In artful wanderings cuts a fair design,
> And leaves long, twisted furrows like a plough . . . .

As he writes, the scribe's "iron point" turns the wax on his tablet over like a plough turning over the earth. The scribe actually inscribes the text; he cuts into the wax. The "furrow" created by the pen becomes the fertile line growing out of the "furrowed brain."

In *North*, the figure of scribe also assumes a slightly more archaic form in the figure of the engraver or scrimshawist in "Viking Dublin: Trial Pieces." The "small outline" that "was incised, a cage / or trellis to conjure in" (1) on bone graphically joins "Viking Dublin: Trial Pieces" to "North." The ploughed furrow of the scribe corresponds to the "incised" image that is cut into the bone.

—Rand Brandes, "'Inscribed in Sheets': Seamus Heaney's Scribal Matrix," *Seamus Heaney: The Shaping Spirit*, Catharine Malloy and Phyllis Carey, eds. (London: Associated University Presses, 1996): pp. 52, 53-54.

CHARLES L. O'NEILL ON HEANEY'S REACTION TO IRELAND'S VIOLENCE

[Charles L. O'Neill has taught at St. Thomas Aquinas College. He has published essays in various journals and has written a regular column for the *Irish Times*. In the following selection, he shows Heaney's need to confront his country's violent past in an effort to understand its still-violent present. O'Neill sees the poems in *North* as espousing the theory that violence is endemic to humanity.]

Published in 1975, Seamus Heaney's *North* remains the most complex and problematic work of art provoked by the renewal of sectarian conflict in Northern Ireland. It has been praised for putting that conflict in a larger mythological perspective as well as criticized for appearing to impute to it a fatalistic historical determinism. By bringing the violence of the past in touch with that of the present, the poems of *North* draw Iron Age, Viking, and modern Irish societies together in a lyric sequence that aspires to mythic resonance. Examining Heaney's myth of "North," a myth that mixes violence, revenge, human sacrifice, and religion, in light of the ideas of nature and culture proposed by the critical theorist, René Girard, may illuminate and extend the images and intuitions Heaney's sequence develops. "Violence," Girard has written, in terms that bring the poems of *North* to mind, "is the heart and secret soul of the sacred." (. . .)

In *Violent Origins*, a collaborative effort by Girard, Burkert, and

Jonathan Z. Smith that treats the origins of culture, the core of Girard's complex theory is explained this way:

> Violence . . . is endemic to human society, and there is no solution to this problem except for the answer that religion gives. Since that answer is given in the rituals of killing and their rationalizations as "sacrifice," the solution that religion provides is also an act of violence. Violence, then, is the manifestation of the Sacred in its dual mode of (1) the terror of uncontrolled killing, and (2) controlled rituals of sacrifice. (6–7) (. . .)

Heaney began his career as a pastoral poet, his first three books evoking the landscapes and immemorial customs of the Northern Irish countryside in which he was raised. The violence that escalated in 1969 between Catholic and Protestant factions had serious imaginative consequences for Heaney's work. "From that moment," he wrote, "the problems of poetry moved from being simply a matter of achieving the satisfactory verbal icon to being a search for images and symbols adequate to our predicament" (*Pr* 56). (. . .)

"North" (*N* 19–20), the title poem of the sequence, dramatizes Heaney's quest for this "originary" violence. It begins thus:

> I returned to a long strand,
> the hammered shod of a bay,
> and found only the secular
> powers of the Atlantic thundering.
>   (19)

But those "secular powers" are soon replaced in Heaney's imagination by "fabulous raiders"—the Vikings—whose "ocean-deafened voices / . . . lifted again / in violence and epiphany." To the poet, "The longship's swimming tongue / was buoyant with hindsight—"; it recalls

> thick-witted couplings and revenges
>
> the hatreds and behindbacks
> of the althing, lies and women,
> exhaustions nominated peace,
> memory incubating the spilled blood.
>   (20)

If "memory"—here subjective individual vision as well as collective unconscious—"incubates" "spilled blood," the poem's "sacred powers" are implicated in violence and revenge. "Violence," Girard writes, "strikes men as an epiphany," and this recognition provides the poem's epiphanic injunction as the voice of the violent past enjoins the modern poet to "Lie down / in the word-hoard," and there, "in the coil and gleam / of your furrowed brain" (20), the poet will find the words and images of the past that precisely define the catastrophic present moment.

—Charles L. O'Neill, "Violence and the Sacred in Seamus Heaney's North," *Seamus Heaney: The Shaping Spirit*, Catharine Malloy and Phyllis Carey, eds. (London: Associated University Presses, 1996): pp. 91-92, 94-95.

"Singing School"

"Singing School" is a collection of six poems that closes the book *North* (1975). The poems describe striking personal occurrences in the artist's life (most of which are based on actual experiences from Heaney's own life) as he struggles to understand himself as poet. More specifically, he must confront his role as Irish writer, who has tight connections to his native land and who is scarred by British control and the violence it has perpetuated. Throughout there is a juxtaposition between driving poetic inspiration and violent and oppressive political circumstance. For Heaney, both must coexist and be understood.

The epigraphs at the poem's opening, selections from Yeats and Wordsworth, and the title of the poem, which also is taken from Yeats, show the narrator placing himself in a respected literary tradition. The "Singing School" title comes from Yeats's poem "Sailing to Byzantium," wherein the singing school provides a disciplined, almost monastic atmosphere seemingly necessary for the poet's existence. In the first poem of the group, "The Ministry of Fear," the narrator is recalling his time at St. Columb's Catholic school where he was a boarder. The place is oppressive and overbearing, where one feels guilty for nearly every act. He is questioned seemingly for no reason both by a priest in school who then hits him as well as by the police who stop him on his way home from a date. The poem contains only a few of the words exchanged; in both cases they are nearly the same—a question of what his name is. From this first poem, then, the poet is confronted, literally, with who he calls himself and he must declare it to others. This school, though, is the place where he and his friend Seamus Deane first create poetry. This provides some liberation.

But repression is not only inflicted upon the young. In the next two poems we see the expansiveness of the British stranglehold on the Irish. In "A Constable Calls," the second of the poems, an officer comes to the narrator's home to record for tax purposes the crops his family has grown. The young narrator, listening to the exchange between his father and the officer, stares at the officer's gun and worries about the one row of turnips the family had planted when the other seed ran out and which his father hasn't reported. The boy imagines the "black hole" of the barracks awaiting them if somehow the authorities find out. The officer rides away, though, unknowing, with his bicycle making a portentous ticking sound, perhaps foreshadowing the ticking bombs that will be used when Ireland's passivity wears out.

The third poem, "Orange Drums, Tyrone, 1966," has Protestant sectarianism showcased in the streets, where a parade honors the triumph of William of Orange. The Catholics are still passive, yet there is an irony, for the drummer described here struggles to carry his instrument. While his side may be in control, he certainly is not, as he fights to hold up the drum, indicating an ability to be weak but still in control or perhaps inspiring the realization in the onlookers that these rulers could be overpowered.

Violence has indeed broken out by the fourth poem, "Summer 1969," but now the narrator is in Spain and is not a participant or eyewitness. His reaction is to study the work of Goya, another artist who struggled with being an artist in a homeland of political chaos. In the first Goya painting the artist sympathizes with the condemned rebels portrayed, and the second depicts the ugly evil of Saturn, who eats his own children. Yet another painting shows two primitive Celtic warriors clubbing each other to death. Violence comes in many forms and none are of value.

Time goes backward after this, for the fifth poem, "Fosterage," takes place in 1962, before the 1969 outbreak. The narrator returns to a more personal occurrence, a meeting with a poet who has been a mentor to the narrator. This mentor advises, "'Description is revelation!'" as the opening to the poem, offering the idea that the poet need not run from the political but can analyze it with fresh eyes, making it new. "Go your own way," the mentor recommends, advocating that the poet can go his own way without it being the way of near total exile, that he can take on politics while still being his own person. The poet's sensitivities can provide revelation, and revelation may bring change.

"Exposure" is the final poem in the collection, its title indicating a vulnerability. There are a number of images of light in this poem. "A comet that was lost / Should be visible at sunset, / Those million tons of light" the poet says, hopeful, for in fact it is near sunset in this poem. Similarly, the light imagery continues when his friends are said to offer "Beautiful prismatic counseling." And while it is December, the time of winter's stasis, and while it is raining, there is hope, still, as well, for "each drop recalls / The diamond absolutes." Since stunning, sparkling "absolutes" are revealed with each drop, self-realization may not be too far off. The "exposure" referred to, then, may be the exposure of the fact that the poet does not know himself, still, and must continue that quest.

CRITICAL VIEWS ON

"Singing School"

EDNA LONGLEY ON THE LACK OF IMPACT IN "SINGING
SCHOOL"

[Edna Longley has been Professor of English at Queen's University, Belfast, and an editor of the *Irish Review*. She has published poems, essays, and some books, including *The Living Stream: Literature & Revisionism in Ireland*. The extract here is from another of her books and points out Heaney's weaknesses in sections of "Singing School," which are at times "melodramatic" and "self-conscious."]

Much of the aggravation continues as a portrait of the artist, especially in the sequence 'Singing School' which begins with 'The Ministry of Fear'. The third poem, 'Orange Drums, Tyrone, 1966', was written before the Troubles—a pointer to how throughout *North* Heaney's creative maturity catches up on his youthful pieties and impieties. Combining aural and visual menace, the drums define Unionist hegemony in terms of 'giant tumours', of a claustrophobic violence that afflicts its inflictor:

> The pigskin's scourged until his knuckles bleed.
> The air is pounding like a stethoscope.

'A Constable Calls' (the second poem) lacks the same ultimate impact, the caller's bike becoming, even from the child's eye view, an implausibly melodramatic time-bomb: 'His boot pushed off / And the bicycle ticked, ticked, ticked.' However, both poems explore their own subjects; we infer the effect on Heaney's developing sensibility. 'The Ministry of Fear' and 'Summer 1969' (4) seem written largely for the sake of the sequence, and to fill in a poetic curriculum vitae (down to the provision of dates). Again, the nods to Yeats and Wordsworth in Heaney's titles and epigraphs (one of which is 'Fair seedtime had my soul') look self-conscious as well as satirical. 'The Ministry of Fear' veers from the sharply specific:

> In the first week
> I was so homesick I couldn't even eat
> The biscuits left to sweeten my exile.
> I threw them over the fence one night
> In September 1951 . . .

to the archly literary: 'It was an act / Of stealth.' Heaney's theme may contrast the boy and the 'sophisticated' author ('Here's two on's are sophisticated'), but his language need not divide them. Also sophisticated, 'Summer 1969' forces home-thoughts from Spain: 'stinks from the fishmarket / Rose like the reek off a flaxdam'; cites Lorca and Goya as exemplars in the context of trying 'to touch the people'; and finally applies too much local colour to the latter's portrait:

> He painted with his fists and elbows, flourished
> The stained cape of his heart as history charged.

This is elementary stuff from the proven matador of *Wintering Out*.

The two remaining poems, 'Fosterage' (5) and 'Exposure' (6), withdraw towards the centre of Heaney's own art. The former quotes the anti-heroic advice of Ulster short-story writer Michael McLaverty ('Don't have the veins bulging in your biro'), although the manner and content of the last line partially disregard it: 'and sent me out, with words / Imposing on my tongue like obols'. 'Exposure' (to which I shall return) sets up a much more genuine inner conflict than 'Summer 1969', and falls a long way short of confidently identifying the artist with the man of action:

> I walk through damp leaves,
> Husks, the spent flukes of autumn,
>
> Imagining a hero
> On some muddy compound,
> His gift like a slingstone
> Whirled for the desperate.

This truly is the doubtful mood and mode of Yeats's 'Meditations in Time of Civil War':

> I turn away and shut the door, and on the stair
> Wonder how many times I could have proved my worth
> In something that all others understand or share.

—Edna Longley, *Poetry in the Wars*, (Newcastle upon Tyne: Bloodaxe Books, 1986): pp. 147-48.

MICHAEL MOLINO ON THE POET'S PLACE

[Michael Molino teaches English at Southern Illinois University, Carbondale. He focuses here on the final poem in "Singing School," wherein the narrator realizes he cannot be the Romantic hero for his country. He therefore must determine what he will be instead, without completely turning his back on his people.]

The final poem in "Singing School" is "Exposure," a poem that does not account for a particular time and place beyond the month of December in Wicklow. The poem is ten quatrains in which the narrator contemplates his role as an artist. The first three stanzas have the flow, imagery and spirit of a Wordsworthian poem: "birches inheriting the last light," "A comet that was lost," and the occasional glimpses of insight. However, the narrator walks along in this pastoral setting only "Imagining a hero." This imagined hero would be a David who could slay the Goliath and save his desperate people:

> Imagining a hero
> On some muddy compound,
> His gift like a slingstone
> Whirled for the desperate.

The narrator realizes that he is not such a hero. All the fosterage he has received, the "Beautiful prismatic counselling," has not rendered such a hero, the romantic poetic hero.

The narrator contemplates his exile and alienation from those friends who are full of passionate intensity. Their counselling is prismatic, abstracted and dispersed light, while others with "anvil brains" hate him because he will not submit to the hammer and anvil that will mould him into the poet hero: "For what? For ear? For the people?" The "ear" is a metonymy of poetics, "People" a metonymy of politics.

In stanza seven, there is a return to the romantic tradition as the rain falls with "Its low conducive voices." The narrator, in

Wordsworthian fashion, experiences the essence of the rain drops that simultaneously evoke the timebound and the timeless:

> Rain comes down through the alders,
> Its low conducive voices
> Mutters about let-downs and erosions
> And yet each drop recalls
>
> The diamond absolutes.

Stanzas eight, nine and ten are one sentence—a sequence of clauses that describe the narrator, a juxtapositioning of images through which the narrator might define himself. The narrator claims that he is neither trapped within (an "internee") nor trapped outside (an "informer" of nature). Stanzas eight through ten are a list of characteristics, albeit coolly ironical, that portray the narrator. He is an emigrant of the mind, escaping political oppression (an exile) and a long-haired thinker. He is also an Irish foot soldier or peasant who has escaped from the massacre and sought solace in the pastoral setting of the forest, one who is "Taking protective colouring / From bole and bark." The reference to the "bole and bark" alludes to Yeats' "Among School Children" and the fact that the artist and the art co-mingle until neither is distinguishable from the other—that is, a total immersion into the artistic sphere, with a consequential loss of personal identity. It appears that the narrator has chosen to follow his artistic calling rather than a political one.

The last stanza is problematic though. Stanza ten begins with the pronoun "Who," which has the antecedent "I," the narrator:

> Who, blowing up these sparks
> For their meager heat, have missed
> The once-in-a-lifetime portent,
> The comet's pulsing rose.

Has the narrator already missed the once-in-a-lifetime portent? If so, then the poem is a lament; surely a once-in-a-lifetime portent cannot be taken lightly. If, however, the poem is a projection of the narrator into the future, his "December" when he is the tattered coat upon a stick, then the poem is a premonition of how his life might be if he follows the Yeatsian path.

—Michael Molino, " Heaney's 'Singing School': A Portrait of the Artist." *The Journal of Irish Literature* 16, no. 3 (September 1987): pp. 15-16.

EAMMON HUGHES ON HEANEY'S STRUGGLE FOR IDENTITY

[Eammon Hughes has been a lecturer in the School of English at Queen's University, Belfast. He is the editor of *Culture and Politics in Northern Ireland, 1960-1990*. The selection here focuses on "The Ministry of Fear" and how Heaney explores the melding of his varied background— Irish, English, Catholic—and his concern with which is the true self.]

'The Ministry of Fear' (*N*, pp. 63–65) is about Heaney's growth as a poet. Addressed to Seamus Deane, it begins with a reference to Kavanagh, and goes on to school life, education and the learning of a variety of voices, but returns to the 'South Derry rhyme' (*N*, p. 64), which locates his voice. The poem matches Heaney's lived experience against an array of 'foreign discourses'. The language in which he registers experience is the language of a poetic tradition which he is constructing. Gazing into 'new worlds' from his school, he echoes Shakespeare; throwing biscuits away becomes a Wordsworthian 'act of stealth'; his first attempts at writing poetry develop, in Kavanagh's terms, into a life (*N*, p. 63). His experiences in school—'inferiority complexes . . . '—and corporal punishment, are both Shakespearean and Joycean (*N*, p. 64). Certain events seemingly cannot be voiced in this way—the growth of sexuality and the encounter with the R.U.C. (*N*, p. 64)—which is consonant with the inability of the English poetic traditions perceived by Heaney to comprehend particular types of experience. He has spoken of the 'insulated and balanced statement . . . that corsetted and decorous truthfulness' towards which 'recent English language' poetry has tended. Although certain issues cannot, apparently, be forced into this tradition, Heaney relies on it to represent the facts of his own life. The name he gives the framework in which he grows, 'the ministry of fear', evokes both Coleridge's 'secret ministry' and Wordsworth's 'ministry / more palpable' in such a way as to suggest the importance of this poetic tradition in Heaney's self-representation.

Heaney, as schoolboy, is 'shying as usual' (*N*, p. 64)—still indulging the reticence of his community. This is not a response to the overwhelming force of English culture. That culture represents a means of expressing himself while still remaining true to the traditions of his community. The poem is an effort to comprehend both the silence of the community and this poetic tradition. 'Ulster was British, but with no rights on / The English lyric . . . ' (*N*, p. 65) is therefore a statement of the situation which Heaney is trying to redress in his very articulation of it.

The poem's 'foreign discourses' can be divided into English and Irish with the Irish voices being apparently more intimate. The latter are just as removed from Heaney as the English ones. Deane, for example, is bewildering. His 'hieroglyphics' are not easily comprehended and his 'svelte dictions' seem almost an embarrassment (*N*, p. 65). Deane's strangeness is balanced by Kavanagh's reminder of the importance of the local, which Heaney both endorses and alters. Heaney's balancing of these two is a mark of his confidence. English poetry, Irish poetry, Catholic schooling, sexuality, and the fear of living in a hostile state are the elements which constitute Heaney's identity in this poem. His confidence rests not in a certainty about how they fit together but in his juxtaposition of them as his identity. (. . .)

Heaney's attitude is not one of being Irish and wanting to be British; nor is it one of being tainted by Britishness and wanting to be pristinely Irish. Rather, he feels himself pulled in two ways. His identity and his voice are not unitary because their determinants are not unitary. This struggle for definition is specifically located in a preoccupied language.

The language issue is a common feature (if any history of colonial dispossession and the reassertion of national rights.

—Eammon Hughes, "Representation in Modern Irish Poetry," *Aspects of Irish Studies*, Myrtle Hill and Sarah Barber, eds. (Belfast: The Queen's University of Belfast, 1990): pp. 58, 59.

LUCY MCDIARMID ON THE STATE VS. THE POET

[Lucy McDiarmid teaches English at Villanova University. She is the author of *Auden's Apologies for Poetry* and has co-edited other literary works. In the following extract, she comments on poems three through six, where the poet wavers between taking a political role or a personal role, and then realizes that the private self cannot escape the world at large.]

The next two poems show the obtrusive Northern Irish state as it is manifested in taxes and parades. The constable who calls to assess the family's taxes works for some ministry of fear, inspiring the young boy's anxiety that his father is hiding other root crops. And the "orange drums," like the constable's bicycle, fill the air with aggression. "Summer 1969" is the first poem to suggest the possibility that the realm of poetry might be used to oppose the State. When the Troubles begin again in 1969, Heaney is in Madrid, reading in the "life of Joyce" about a writer who stands as a model of minding his own aesthetic business in spite of Irish troubles. But the kind of voice that always appears in Heaney's poems to tell him what to do (like the longboat's swimming tongue in "North," or the ghost of Joyce at the end of *Station Island*) urges political engagement: "Go back . . . try to touch the people." Heaney's reaction is typically cautious: he "retreated to the cool of the Prado" to look at paintings of political events, such as Goya's *Shootings of the Third of May*. In lines Edna Longley calls the "elementary stuff from the proven matador" (71), Heaney characterizes painting as activism: "He painted with his fists and elbows, flourished / The stained cape of his heart as history charged." The unconvincing diction suggests that this possibility is rejected even as it is articulated.

"Fosterage," the next poem, offers another option in another absolute voice: "'Description is revelation.'" Heaney's former teaching colleague, the writer Michael McLaverty, dominates a classroom in the same singing school, a room somewhat closer to Byzantium: "'Listen. Go your own way. / Do your own work.'" Quoting Katherine Mansfield and citing Hopkins, neither of whom are notably engagé writers, McLaverty "gripped my elbow" and "fostered me and sent me out." Fosterage offers a more affectionate and personal mode of teaching than the priest with his whip, a mode that situates the relation of teacher to student in the private space of friendship rather than the civic space of the RUC. McLaverty's recommendation of artistic autonomy suggests that the poet can define his relation to ideologies in any way he desires. It's significant, however, that "fosterage" does not take place in an actual classroom but outdoors on a weekend ("Royal / Avenue, Belfast, 1962, / A Saturday afternoon"). The surrounding walls of a classroom would be inconsistent with such a liberating view.

"Exposure," the final and best poem in *Singing School*, begins in a private, contemplative moment: "It is December in Wicklow." In exile like Ovid, Heaney sits "weighing and weighing / My responsible *tristia.*" He appears to have taken McLaverty's advice but to have discovered that it isn't possible to "go your own way" as if ideological conflict could be ignored. Even in retreat in the southern part of Ireland, "escaped," responsibility weighs him down; so, like Yeats, he makes poetry out of ambivalence and guilt.

—Lucy McDiarmid, "Heaney and the Politics of the Classroom," *Critical Essays on Seamus Heaney*, Robert F. Garratt, ed. (New York: G. K. Hall & Co., 1995): pp. 116-17.

CRITICAL ANALYSIS OF THE

"Glanmore Sonnets"

The "Glanmore Sonnets," a collection of ten sonnets, lie at the near center of *Field Work* (published in 1979) and serve as the transition in the book. The book's beginning in many ways is a continuation of public and political themes from Heaney's previous work, *North*. But the sonnets create a switch, returning to the hope that convening with nature and one's personal self will provide an escape from the strife of the current situation in Heaney's Ireland. The concern with nature and the personal is similar to that expressed in Heaney's earlier poetry, but here there is a new twist, for now nature and the private contemplative poet merge with the larger public world. The poems are written about a four-year period when Heaney lived with his family in the countryside of Glanmore. They moved there from Belfast in an attempt not only to escape the continuing violence in Northern Ireland but so that Heaney could renew his poetic self and return to his roots, since this place is similar to where he lived in his young years.

The first sonnet mixes description of growth and fertility with allusions to art and the creative process. "Vowels ploughed into other: opened ground" is the first line, where the vowels are in charge, forging a space for themselves, seemingly to create the right place where growth can occur, where other sounds can be planted as well. The sonnet is brimming with vitality and the ploughing is intense, deep. Even though it is February, it is the mildest one for twenty years, the acres "breathe," the earth is "new," and the ploughs "gorge" not just the land but into the subsoil.

By the seventh line Heaney calls "art a paradigm of earth new from the lathe." He says that his own lea (meaning grassland or meadow) is "deeply tilled," and one assumes his "lea" is not only literally these meadows they are now living amongst, but his fertile place of creativity from which his poetry grows. The plough has reached all of his senses, and he describes himself as inspired, saying "I am quickened." Yet there is a pause and shift in the last three lines of the sonnet, where Heaney literally tells the reader to stop. His ghosts have appeared, not frightening ghosts but ones that do disturb his moment. We assume these ghosts are old thoughts, old methods of creating, old distractions, even, and the poem ends by comparing this disturbance to "freakish Easter snows," unpredictable yet still not preventing the occurrence of Spring. But they are not described as Spring snows but as Easter snows, giving them more gravity by the religious reference to a miraculous resurrection from the dead.

Sonnet II starts with words, not just the vowels that were at the beginning of the first sonnet. Words are coming forth from the darkness of the poet's depths. Then, the birth is interrupted by a quote: "These things are not secrets but mysteries." We find out that the quote comes from a sculptor, who spoke to the narrator some time ago. Parts of life will never be understood, he is saying, although many don't recognize this and keep searching to try to find answers. As he speaks he is chiseling at a piece of stone. The narrator describes the stone as working with the chisel and the mallet to create the final art. The tools, raw material, and sculptor are as one.

Now, the narrator says, he is in the "hedge-school of Glanmore." This description refers to the schools that the Irish Catholics created out under the trees and alongside the hedges in the nineteenth century before formal education was allowed for them. It refers not only to the narrator's wanting to learn from the nature available in Glanmore but also refers to political rebelliousness.

The third sonnet continues like its predecessors with a thorough appreciation of the natural surroundings and with a merging of these surroundings and poetry. The setting is described as "iambic," for example, and later a breeze "Is cadences." But, again, there is an interruption of the blissful observances with a quote, but this time it is a quote of the narrator himself, something he had said earlier to his wife. He says of their surroundings "I won't relapse / From this strange loneliness I've brought us to." It is a mixed reaction—a seeming attraction to the land that he wants to encourage, a realization that it is even more full of mystery than he expected, and a wondering that perhaps this exile is too much to impose on his whole family. Then he goes on to compare he and his wife to Dorothy and William Wordsworth, and before he can finish, his wife interrupts him and tells him not to continue. She is reality imposing on his dream, pushing back on his over-blown view of himself. But immediately after this interruption, the narrator returns to his dream-like amazement over nature.

Sonnets IV and V follow the Wordsworthian tradition of childhood reminiscences. For Heaney, there is a need to return to his roots, to what has been innately his since birth. In sonnet IV he thinks about what makes him different. For example, while others have said they could tell an approaching train by putting an ear to the tracks, this narrator has never done it that way but has been able to tell by other natural occurrences, such as the "head / Of a horse swirled back from a gate." In sonnet V he warmly remembers a tree from his childhood: "I love its blooms like saucers brimmed with meal, / Its berries . . . light bruised out of purple." The memory is beautiful, but at the same time it recalls a friction, albeit one that is quite underlying and one that seems to have been accepted. For "boortree" is what the Irish call the tree, while the English call it "edlderberry," and so the narrator has almost begrudgingly "learned to call it." He has been taught both names, and both backgrounds have mixed inside himself: the English Wordsworthian tradition and sonnet form and his innate Irish heritage. Even though he is out in the solitary countryside, the English / Irish conflict still exists.

In sonnet VI the narrator looks curiously at an event from 1947 when a man attempted to race his bike across the frozen Moyola River. He explains how they were excited by the man and his daredevilry, calling him a "wild white goose," and contrasts his courage and free spirit with the safety of their quiet home.

Sonnet VII also looks back at a time of youth. The narrator recalls listening on the radio to the announcements of gale warnings in coastal towns of Northern Ireland. He lists their names both at the poem's opening and again lists more names at its very close. He appreciates the sounds of their names, as well as sounds of the names of the French ships that would take refuge in harbors while the storms passed. He recalls an appreciation of the marvels of nature, and, as in the previous sonnet, an appreciation of the comforts of being inside, this time in his childhood's kitchen, gathered around the radio.

Sonnet VIII also starts with a storm. Here it is lighting a pile of split logs, but the feeling is completely different than that in the previous sonnet. Here there are overwhelming fears, omens, unknown evils, death. Many of the lines are trembling questions, repeatedly wondering what danger is to come. Then there is a longer question, addressed to his wife, asking her to remember his vivid image of an older woman who they had seen years ago comforting a young child with her singing, hugging, and rocking. The sonnet ends with two powerful, intimate lines to his wife: "Come to me quick, I am upstairs shaking. / My all of you birchwood in lightning." He looks to her for comfort from the terror of his anxiety. He now is the wood from the first line, exposed to the lightning. He and she mix in the "My all of you" description.

In Sonnet IX there again is ugliness and blood. "Did we come to the wilderness for this?" the poet asks when he sees the black rat that his wife wants him to kill, dangling, seemingly tauntingly, on a swaying branch outside his kitchen window. Yet when the narrator arrives outside the rat is gone and he asks, "What is my apology for poetry?" He questions if he is doing the right thing when, for the sake of becoming a stronger poet, he keeps his family out in this wilderness that he is now seeing as more and more wild. He uses James Joyce's word "inwit," which comes from a phrase he created to mean "remorse of conscience." At the same time, though, what his wife perceived as a threat has disappeared. He turns to see her now through the window, comparing her face to "a new moon glimpsed through tangled glass." But in reality a new moon is seldom visible, except for possibly a thin crescent section at sunset. Also, the description refers to old folklore wherein it is considered bad luck to see a new moon through glass.

The final sonnet is much calmer. The narrator describes a dream he had of he and his wife sleeping in a moss under blankets. He compares them to lovers from works of literature—two from England's Shakespeare and two from Irish mythology—but both pairs being fugitives in danger of losing their lives. He describes his own surprise at having dreamed of the first night he and his wife were together, remembering her "deliberate kiss," and then "our separateness; / The respite in our dewy dreaming faces." It is a strong, positive, intimate ending for the entire "Glanmore Sonnets" sequence.

Heaney would later describe the family's time in Glanmore as having renewed him in numerous ways. While it could not provide an escape from the troubles of Ireland, it could and did provide a respite. It also provoked a renewed understanding that beauty and calm can coexist with darkness and fragility, that the private can never be separate from the public, and that the natural world and man's created world of art/poetry are enmeshed.

"Glanmore Sonnets"

NEIL CORCORAN ON HEANEY'S REMINDER OF SUFFERING

[Neil Corcoran has been Professor of English at the University of Wales, Swansea. He has written books on poetry, including *After Yeats & Joyce: Reading Modern Irish Literature*. He has also edited two books on poetry. Here he tells us that for all the comfort and calm of the "Glanmore Sonnets" they contain a continued reminder of the world's pain and our vulnerability to it.]

[T]hese are all poems which manage to 'say' complex experiences, even while reminding us of the difficulty with which any experience struggles out of its 'hiding place' into the articulation of a poem. Made partly out of other poems, and gratefully allusive to them, the 'Glanmore Sonnets' are nevertheless directed out towards the world as well as inwards towards literature itself, seeking their ideal in a harmoniously reciprocal relationship between art and nature, language and experience. The sequence discovers its finest metaphor for these correspondences not in literary creation, but in sculpture, when, in II, Oisin Kelly is imagined 'hankering after stone / That connived with the chisel, as if the grain / Remembered what the mallet tapped to know.'

An understanding of these relationships, however, is not simply given, it must be slowly acquired; and this is why Glanmore is a 'hedge-school' in which Heaney can learn a voice that might 'continue, hold, dispel, appease'. The 'hedge-schools' were the only means the native Irish had of gaining an education during the period of the Penal Laws, and we can take it that what this voice must dispel and appease is, at least in part, the inheritance of a history of violence and repression (the original title of the sequence, for a limited edition, was in fact *Hedge School*). For all that the sonnets find their comforts in 'pastoral' calm, in literature, and in the achieved mutuality of marriage, these consolations are set in their fragility against insistent reminders of the world's pain. In VIII, the innocent sight of a magpie inspecting a sleeping horse summons to mind the 'armour and carrion' of a historical battlefield; in IX, a rat 'Sways on the briar like infected fruit', terrifying the poet's wife, and other rats killed in threshing leave their 'Blood on a pitch-fork, blood on chaff and hay'; and the final sonnet evokes a dream in which husband and wife lie down together and apart, in the attitude of death, as well as the embrace of sexual love.

In 'Yeats as an Example?' in *Preoccupations*, Heaney claims that, in Yeats's poems, 'the finally exemplary moments are those when [the] powerful artistic control is vulnerable to the pain or pathos of life itself. The strength of the 'Glanmore Sonnets' is that, for all the control of their artistry, and the self-delight of their literariness, they never forget this vulnerability. I think of their most characteristic, as well as 'exemplary', moments, then, as the conclusions of sonnets VIII and X. Sonnet VIII:

> Do you remember that pension in *Les Landes*
> Where the old one rocked and rocked and rocked
> A mongol in her lap, to little songs?
> Come to me quick, I am upstairs shaking.
> My all of you birchwood in lightning.

The poignant memory of human suffering there is countered with the urgent imperative of sexual desire, as if the one could occlude the other. It is the vulnerable desperation which registers most powerfully, however, in the phrase 'My all of you', which effects a grammatical conjunction (of his possessive adjective and her personal pronoun) responsively imitative of the sexual conjunction itself, in which he will be taken over, possessed, taken out of himself, like the wood devoured by lightning. That 'all' rivals, in the sheer force of its plenitude, some Joycean uses of the word: Bloom in 'Lestrygonians', for instance ('Perfume of embraces all him assailed. With hungered flesh obscurely, he mutely craved to adore'), or Joyce himself in a letter to Nora of 22 August 1909 ('Give yourself to me, dearest, all, all when we meet'). It also perhaps remembers the concluding line of 'Oysters', with its hope that the day's tang 'Might quicken me all into verb, pure verb'. It is the humbled expression of overwhelming need, as well as of irresistible desire.

—Neil Corcoran, *Seamus Heaney*, (London: Faber and Faber Limited, 1986): pp. 146-48.

[Deborah McLoughlin has taught at Rochdale College and edited the Arnold edition of Jean Rhys's *Wide Sargasso Sea*. In this selection she describes Heaney's belief that his new life in Glanmore would be a wonderful respite. In reality, while his time here is full of love and sweetness, it also is a period of profound guilt and awareness of the continued suffering in the North he's abandoned.]

If Sonnet IX represents the climax of the poet's ominous insecurity, Sonnet X is a calmer denouement which ends the sequence on a tentative note of repose. In it Heaney has a dream vision of himself and Marie as lovers asleep "in a moss" ("moss" is the Irish word for bog). Heaney's first home was called Mossbawn, and so the locale carries connotations of familiarity and security which are immediately undermined by Heaney's choice of role models: "Lorenzo and Jessica in a cold climate. / Diarmuid and Grainne waiting to be found." These two pairs of lovers—one from Shakespeare, and one from Irish myth—represent Heaney's acknowledgement that he draws on both English and Irish traditions, but both pairs are fugitives in imminent danger of losing their lives. The words used to describe the sleeping lovers, "asperged, . . . censed, . . . effigies," collocate to convey a deathly atmosphere which is temporarily dissipated by Heaney's recollection of his and Marie's first night together. Their lovemaking is a sacramental raising towards "covenants of flesh"; an ecstasy whose fragility is highlighted by the allusion to Wyatt, implicit in the phrase, "How like you this?" Heaney is quoting from Wyatt's "They fle from me that sometyme did me seke," written shortly after his patron Thomas Cromwell was executed, and the poet's subsequent social ostracism. Wyatt was actually arrested six months after writing the poem, which includes the tenderly erotic lines:

> And she me caught in her armes long and small;
> Therewithall swetely did me kysse,
> And softley said, dere hert, howe like you this?

Heaney's sonnet is faithful to the tenderness of the English lyric, but Wyatt is also here as an admonitory example of how poets may become victims of political pressures and turbulence.

This final sonnet balances private love against public fear, haven with exile, and life with living death to conclude with a vision of peace achieved through mutual love, "The respite in our dewy dreaming faces," whose transience is implicit in "respite." A key word here is "dewy": at the conclusion of Canto I of the *Purgatorio* Virgil cleanses Dante's face with dew of the tears he shed in hell in preparation for their ascent of Mount Purgatory. Heaney has translated and adapted the passage in another *Fieldwork* poem, "The Strand at Lough Beg," and it would not be entirely fanciful to detect the ghost of its presence here. Heaney had clearly sensed the possibility of paradise at Glanmore, but the reality has been of a series of infernal intimations, and of a paradise postponed. Sonnet X, with its tentative definition of paradise as moments of respite, seems to be a realistic reproach of the facility with which he had prefigured his pastoral idyll in Sonnet I:

> Now the good life could be to cross a field
> And art a paradigm of earth new from the lathe
> Of ploughs.

The "dreaming faces" of Heaney and his wife recall the "dream grain" sown in Sonnet 1, but its germination in Heaney's imagination has produced a crop of guilt, terror, and doubt as well as the anticipated love and pastoral sweetness. Heaney had predicted as much with his paradoxical image of the seed whirling "like freakish Easter snows" promising renewal, while at the same time attesting that he will not and cannot abandon the glacial world which he had conceived and depicted in *North*.

The parallel between Heaney's mood here and Yeats's disparaging reference to the life of the poet as the "cold snows of a dream" is central to this sequence which may be received as Heaney's own "Meditations in Time of Civil War." Heaney shares with Yeats guilt at a failure to be more "involved," and there are other elements common to both: a sense of the primacy of domestic love, an appreciation of natural surroundings, an acknowledgement of the importance of the poet's place within a cultural tradition. The tension between Heaney's eagerness to express love and "sweetness" and his need to attend to messages from a brutal beyond is a vivifying element in these simultaneously beautiful and disturbing poems. They articulate Heaney's ever-present consciousness of the suffering in the North to which his absence makes him all the more keenly attentive. They also voice his sometimes sustaining, sometimes enervating awareness of what other poets have been, said, done, and felt in circumstances of personal stress and national trauma.

> —Deborah McLoughlin, "'An Ear to the Line': Modes of Receptivity in Seamus Heaney's 'Glanmore Sonnets,'" *Papers on Language and Literature* 25, no. 2 (Spring 1989): pp. 213-215.

Sidney Burris on Heaney's Wordsworthian Childhood Vision

[Sidney Burris has been Assistant Professor of English at the University of Arkansas. He has won the Academy of American Poets Prize and written a collection of poetry, *A Day at the Races* (1989). In the following piece, he analyzes the fourth of the "Glanmore Sonnets." Here he remarks on Heaney's return to childhood methods of learning and reasoning, in the hope that they can offer the poet a trusted means of responding to his country's current violence.]

Childhood, or rather, an artful version of childhood's innocence, remoteness, and simplicity, fuels many nostalgic visions, and even Yeats, the promenading Irishman who claimed to remember "little of childhood but its pain," crowded the first chapter of his *Autobiography* with highly enameled recollections of Sligo, a place that he in fact rarely visited. The fourth sonnet of the sequence alone represents the reconciliatory aspects of pastoral writing and supplies the thematic transition to the various versions of pastoral love that end the sequence. Heaney begins the fourth sonnet with a storyteller's verbal construction, one that, more often than not, signals the advent of a fond recollection:

I used to lie with an ear to the line
For that way, they said, there should come a sound
Escaping ahead, an iron tune
Of flange and piston pitched along the ground,
But I never heard that. Always, instead,
Struck couplings and shuntings two miles away
Lifted over the woods. The head
Of a horse swirled back from a gate, a grey
Turnover of haunch and mane, and I'd look
Up to the cutting where she'd soon appear.
Two fields back, in the house, small ripples shook
Across our drinking water
(As they are shaking now across my heart)
And vanished into where they seemed to start.

After the extensive aesthetic and domestic orientations of the first three sonnets—settling into the cottage and establishing the inspirational possibilities of rural seclusion—the fourth sonnet begins the middle section. Here, Heaney outlines a childhood experience that ultimately concerns an epistemological matter—how he might know for certain that a train was approaching. The conventional wisdom, introduced by the formulaic phrase, "they said," I advised putting his head to the tracks to hear "the flange and piston pitched along the ground," a sound Heaney never heard. Instead, he watched "the head/Of a horse swirled back," and remarks that "two fields back," an innately rural way of giving directions, the drinking water shook with "small ripples." The horse and the water bucket are the harbingers that Heaney best understands because they are more personal, more intuitive, in kind than the humming tracks that intrude, like the "gargling tractors" of the first sonnet, on Heaney's home. The nationalistic, less personal nuances embedded in the second and third sonnets are answered by the intensely personal epistemology erected in the fourth. Faced with the political implications of his domestic exile, Heaney calls upon a childhood experience, a nostalgic vision, to assure him of his intuitive powers. Because they seem pristinely aboriginal, these intuitive powers provide a cogent response to the political conundrums plaguing both Heaney's life and his poetry. It is as if Heaney were searching for an unimpeachable authority, a place from which to begin again; and in this endeavor, Heaney, like most modern writers, inherits the Wordsworthian vision of childhood. These childlike methods of reasoning and learning were, at the very least, innocent of their responsibilities to the larger society, and when the political or social problems of that society weaken the writer's artistic convictions, the writer returns imaginatively to a time when such problems did not exist. Praising the intuitions of childhood is a nostalgic endeavor. Their priority, for the pastoral writer, argues for their persuasiveness.

—Sidney Burris, *The Poetry of Resistance: Seamus Heaney and the Pastoral Tradition*, (Athens: Ohio University Press, 1990): pp. 128-29.

ARTHUR E. MCGUINNESS ON HEANEY'S INABILITY TO FIND PEACE

[Arthur E. McGuinness has been Professor of English at the University of California at Davis. He is the author of *Seamus Heaney: Poet & Critic* as well as other essays on Anglo-Irish writers. His essay shows the "Glanmore Sonnets" as revealing Heaney's attempts to find serenity in nature and instead having to look to voices from his past for consolation.]

The "Glanmore Sonnets," placed immediately after "Elegy," constitute Heaney's first sustained response to Lowell's challenge to be a forger. Set in the "wilderness" place where he has moved with his family, the sonnets are crafted like those "heart-hammering" sonnets of Lowell's *The Dolphin*. Heaney had left Mossbawn and Belfast, familiar rural and urban places in Northern Ireland, for self-imposed exile in Co. Wicklow. He does not feel at home in Glanmore. The place does not provide comforting soundings. Surrounded by a landscape which remains mysterious, his only consolations come from "ghosts," voices from the past which help him relate to the present: the sculptor Oisin Kelly (II), his wife Marie's voice (III), the remembered sound of a train (IV), a speaking tree (V), place-names from the far-flung borders of Ireland (VII), his wife's voice again (IX), and his wife's wedding-night kiss (X). Other orienting "voices" will speak to the poet in both *Field Work* and

Station Island, culminating with the "voices" of James Joyce and Sweeney. These "voices" replace the comforting voice of Mother Earth which spoke to Heaney in his early poems.

The conflict between incubation and forging is manifest in the first of the "Glanmore Sonnets." The poem begins in a familiar landscape which is soon "made strange." The setting at first seems vintage Heaney: "Vowels ploughed," "opened ground," "mist bands over furrows," "distant gargling tractors," "turned-up acres," "the lathe of ploughs" (33). One hears echoes here of "Digging," the first poem in his first published collection, *Death of a Naturalist* (1966). But this familiar rural language no longer inspires the poet. The formula seems to work briefly and gives Heaney a moment of Yeatsian vision: "I am quickened with a redolence / Of the fundamental dark unblown rose." But then the vision fades and is replaced by "ghosts": "Wait then ... Breasting the mist, in sower's aprons, / My ghosts come striding into their spring stations / The dream grain whirls like freakish Easter snows." These "striding" ghosts are forgers rather than incubators.

The first of these ghosts, Oisin Kelly, speaks about secrets and mysteries: "These things are not secrets but mysteries" (34). Secrets can be discovered, if one is patient or sensitive enough. Mysteries can never be understood, but only wondered at and accepted. Heaney's incubation poems have often pondered secrets. But his new landscape, his "wilderness" at Glanmore, remains a mystery. His customary "soundings" are no longer efficacious.

> Then I landed in the hedge-school of Glanmore
> And from the backs of ditches hoped to raise
> A voice caught back off slug-horn and slow chanter
> That might continue, hold, dispel, appease.

His hope for such an enabling voice is not fulfilled. The place remains mysterious.

The voice in Sonnet III, the poet's wife, has no more consolation than Oisin Kelly. Heaney's wife speaks a truth the poet is not prepared for. She says, "You're not going to compare us two ... ?" The unfinished line would read: "to Dorothy and William Wordsworth." Just previously, the poet has said to his wife, "I won't relapse / From this strange loneliness I've brought us to. / Dorothy and William ... " (35). Like the older Wordsworth, Heaney has lost touch with his natural environment, which no longer reveals its secrets. The poet observes natural things around him, the baby rabbit and the deer, but is not transported by the experience, feeling instead a "strange loneliness." Wordsworth's loss of vision was not compounded by alienation from his sister Dorothy. But Heaney gets no consoling words from his wife.

—Arthur E. McGuinness, "Seamus Heaney: The Forging Pilgrim," *Essays in Literature* 18, no. 1 (Spring 1991): pp.50-51.

MICHAEL PARKER ON MERGING TRADITIONS IN THE "GLANMORE SONNETS"

[Michael Parker has been Senior Lecturer in English at the Liverpool Institute of Higher Education. He is the author of *The Hurt World: Short Stories of the Troubles* and a reviewer of poetry, fiction, and drama. The following section from his book on Heaney covers sonnets V, VI, and VII. In discussing sonnet V, he points out Heaney's appreciation for the differing languages and traditions that effected his upbringing. In the two sonnets that follow, he sees Heaney as chastising himself but now determined to take more risks.]

In V he reoccupies imaginatively the 'boortree' bower of his first home, to play a new variation of an old game, 'touching tongues'. From this vantage point 'in the throat' of the tree, he examines the distinctive textures of the two languages and traditions that shaped his upbringing, the intimate native tongue of Mossbawn and the more formal, extended register of language acquired at St Columb's and Queen's. Saying the dialect word, naming the *boortree*, can still evoke its 'soft corrugations', its 'green young shoots' and 'greenish, dank' security, yet the sharpness of these images suffers under the influence of time and the 'alien' tongue. Like the disappearing Gaelic culture mourned in the place-name poems of *Wintering Out*, it is reduced to being only a 'snapping memory', displaced by its English 'equivalent'. (. . .)

Despite his clear preference for the 'bruised' language of home, Heaney is not insensible to the benefits that derived from that other culture. The poem is itself an act of grafting, setting into sensual 'Irish' stock linguistic slivers from his 'English' education, 'cultivated' words such as 'corrugations', 'swart', 'caviar', 'etymologist'. Exile, after all, provided him with the words and forms with which to articulate his *desiderium nostrorum*.

Guilt—perhaps over his present lyric 'truancy', and past reticence on political matters—surfaces again-in the somewhat oblique sixth sonnet. Having ended the previous poem retreating into a foetal position in 'the tree-house' of Mossbawn/Glanmore, Heaney reproaches himself for his 'timid circumspect involvement', determining in a future tense to 'break through . . . what I glazed over', to take more risks. He is quickened by the memory of an anonymous, local act of heroism from the winter of 1947, when a man 'dared the ice/ And raced his bike across the Moyola river'. This tale of bravery, retold 'after dark', generates another childhood recollection in the next sonnet. Just before 'Midnight and closedown', he would listen to the litany of names from the BBC weather forecast—'Dogger, Rockall, Malin, Shetland, Faroes, Finisterre'—and picture awesome, mysterious regions, inhabited solely by keening winds. In contrast to these exposed spaces, possessed for long periods by 'Green, swift upsurges' of natural violence, are 'the lee' and leas 'of Wicklow', which Heaney had made his 'haven'.

—Michael Parker, *Seamus Heaney: The Making of a Poet* (Iowa City: University of Iowa Press, 1993): pp. 169-70..

"The Harvest Bow"

"The Havest Bow" (published in 1979 in *North*) starts seemingly as a warm reminiscence. The "you" described in the poem's first line, who the narrator remembers as braiding a simple bow from straw, is not clearly identified, even by the poem's end. This person could be a woman, since she quietly works at the creation of a bow, work that might stereotypically be relegated to females. As the poem progresses, one could assume that the person described could be an early lover. For in the first stanza, the bow is described as a "love-knot," and later the poet/narrator says he is "homesick" for the evenings spent walking with this unidentified person, passing, among other things, "old beds" in hedges. From other descriptions in the poem, some have assumed the "you" is someone from an earlier generation; Heaney himself, when queried, said his intention was that the person be his father.

From the start, the poem is a mix of positives and negatives. The first of its five stanzas describes the plaiter as having "implicated" his "mellowed silence" in the wheat. "Implicated" literally means to twist or twine into, so the father is weaving parts of his self into this bow. As the description of the memory continues, the wheat, curiously, is first described for an attribute not that it has but an attribute that it does not have and that one would never expect it to have: it "does not rust." We are told, positively, not only of how bright it is but that it actually gets brighter, as if it is almost other-worldly, sacred, eternal. Yet there is some negativity in the poem as well. For while twisting is necessary to the task at hand, there is a tension and almost squiriming that could be the reaction of the reader as we hear of how the bow "tightens twist by twist." By the last line, we have a description that is both positive and negative. Here the bow is a "love-knot," combining both the positive associations of love, as well as the negative associations of a knot. Also, we get the negative description of it as a "throwaway." Love, even in the form of an unrustable knot, is easily expendable in this poem.

By the second stanza, the father is described as hands and fingers that have aged, having worked "a liftetime" in the fields. After this are the third and fourth lines that may refer to his past work in the fields or to the more current reminiscing about the bow-making. Perhaps it is both, as the lines describe the man's hands as having "Harked to their gift and worked with fine intent." Here "gift" refers possibly to the bow that becomes a gift or to the gift he has for working with the earth. Similarly, the description of applying himself "with fine intent" could refer to his work with the bow or his years in the fields. We are told that the man can work (again, no matter which work is being referred to) in a "somnambulant" state. This could show that the work is so natural for him that he can even do it in his sleep, or this could show his own tiredness and possibly advancing age.

In the last couplet of the stanza, "I" is first introduced. We see here a connection between the somnambulant father, eyes closed, that was described above and the description in this couplet of the braille-reading narrator, who also cannot see. Yet the narrator not only can read the braille-like message from the bow and the fields, but he will "tell" it, even though it has been "unsaid." This refers to the role of the poet, who is sensitive enough to observe and gifted enough to be able to effectively relay that observation to the world at large.

But in the two stanzas that follow the second, the narrator goes back even further in time. In these stanzas, he conjours images of an easy, peaceful past. This is brought on by spying into the golden loops of the bow, which seems to take on an almost ethereal quality. There is simple, pastoral beauty in the images, but there is also the more modern railway and the footprint of a harsh reality breaking in, symbolized in the auction notice posted on not the door of a house but on an outhouse wall, again a symbol of a simpler past that may be disappearing. The easy pleasure of waving a stick through the tall weeds and brush even loses its appeal here, "as your stick / Whacking the tips off weeds and bushes / Beats out of time, and beats, but flushes / Nothing . . . ." The stick is seen as destructive to nature, incapable but still trying to keep a beat and able to flush nothing out of its hiding. The breaking of the lines so that the word

"Nothing" appears on the line following the description, adds emphasis to it, as does the colon after it that makes the reader stop.

The end of the fourth stanza returns to the idea of troubled communication. The full last two lines read: "Nothing: that original townland / Still tongue-tied in the straw tied by your hand." Just as the moving stick was unable to produce anything from the growth of the land, so, too, there is a voice that does not come out of the land. The older generation has not passed down to the next a clear path with instructions, but they have left the land, their skills, and their own art in such items as the harvest bow.

The last stanza brings us back to the present, where the narrator speaks of the straw bow that has been pinned up and has inspired his thoughts. This stanza contains the line from Yeats that now makes Heaney's poem more than a personal memory: *"The end of art is peace."* This line illicits thoughts on death, the role of the poet, his relation to others and to politics, as well as the political strife in Heaney's own Northern Ireland. Perhaps Heaney is saying that when the older generation stops communicating and creating it can be at peace and even die, knowing it has done all it could. When the art of the growing field has reached its peak, there is the harvest, and even then there is beauty that can be made out of the smallest remains, the whole poem seems to be saying.

Out of an old, crumbling world, the poet has to make something. Especially for Ireland, where so much strife has taken place, the old, though, must not be allowed to crumble. Poets and others cannot be tongue-tied. For if art stops, the peace we are left with could be death. As the older generation reaches toward rest, the younger generation must become the father and keep the world learning, challenged.

CRITICAL VIEWS ON
"The Harvest Bow"

SIDNEY BURRIS ON HEANEY'S ACCEPTANCE OF TRADITION'S SYMBOLISM

[Here Burris states that whereas previously Heaney was intent on revising pastoral tradition, in "The Harvest Bow" he embraces pastoral symbolism and the "consoling perfections of the past." The poem also reaches beyond the personal, Burris says, in that it connects the viability of poetry with society's state.]

"The Harvest Bow," written in unobtrusive couplets, three to a stanza, is not a seduction piece and does not dwell exclusively, erotically, on the excitements of the present moment. The poem begins in recollection. (...)

The final three stanzas of the poem begin with nostalgic vision of young love and end with a social decree, and the transition between the two depends upon the changing functions of the harvest bow:

> And if I spy into its golden loops
> I see us walk between the railway slopes
> Into an evening of long grass and midges,
> Blue smoke straight up, old beds and ploughs in hedges.
> An auction notice on an outhouse wall—
> You with a harvest bow in your lapel,
>
> Me with the fishing rod, already homesick
> For the big lift of these evenings, as your stick
> Whacking the tips off weeds and bushes
> Beats out of time, and beats, but flushes
> Nothing: that original townland
> Still tongue-tied in the straw tied by your hand.
>
> *The end of art is peace*
> Could be the motto of this frail device
> That I have pinned up on our deal dresser—
> Like a drawn snare
> Slipped lately by the spirit of the corn
> Yet burnished by its passage, and still warm.

The poem moves quickly from a narration of a past incident to a narration of a past incident *remembered*, from the narrative voice to the recollective voice; the evening recalled is one "of long grass and midges," and the poet is "already homesick / For the big lift of these evenings." Intensely personal, the memory triggered by the harvest bow engenders a less personal, more social pronouncement: "*The end of art is peace.*" Perhaps this is a private peace, an individual contentment, but the emotions that lie behind that maxim, and that ultimately give rise to it, draw their strength from a past framed by the "golden loops" of the bow; national—rely on a pastoral historiography that emphasizes the consoling perfections of the past.

The loops of the harvest bow stand in stark contrast to the torc tightened around the Tollund Man; the radical revisions of pastoral nostalgia that Heaney to the Tollund Man's torc have been replaced by an acceptance of the tradition's standard symbols. Complacency often provides an occasion for indiscriminate acceptance, but Heaney's version of Wicklow, where he and his family lived for four years after leaving Belfast, descends from his version of the Irish Free State, the twenty-six counties lying south of Northern Ireland. The poems do not extol the political entity known as the Irish Republic; they offer, as traditional pastoral offers, an imaginative interlude, a consoling vision of the rural society that provides an attractive alternative to the life the poet flees. In this case, the political assignations of these two societies are English and Irish In their governments. But the nostalgia of the verse, while it seems to be innocuous in its ramblings, provides the foundation for a larger statement, a credo of sorts, that links the prosperity of art to the well-being, the peace, of the poet's society.

—Sidney Burris, *The Poetry of Resistance: Seamus Heaney and the Pastoral Tradition*, (Athens: Ohio University Press, 1990): pp. 122-23.

TONY CURTIS SEES IRELAND'S NEED FOR HOPE

[Tony Curtis has been Senior Lecturer in English at the Polytechnic of Wales. He has published and broadcast widely and his poetry has won a number of awards. His books include *How Poets Work* and his own books of poetry. In the following excerpt, he explains Heaney's view that while there may seem to be no clear wisdom from the Irish elders, the poet himself and Ireland can learn from what does survive. Poets should be responsible for keeping it alive.]

'The Harvest Bow' is a tightly-wrought poem, its form complementing the central image. There are five stanzas of six lines, rhyming or half-rhyming in couplets. Internal rhyme and assonance are also used to create a woven form. Heaney is returning to one of his constant themes: the corn-dolly, the "throwaway, love-knot of straw" that represents his heritage. It twists and binds together the knowledge held by "Hands that aged round ashplants and cane sticks/And lapped the spurs on a lifetime of game cocks" and sustains "their gift" which "does not rust". In the context of Ireland the sense of continuance, permanence, a simple strength, is central to the survival of any real hope. There is a sense in which the older man becomes the wheat. He can be seen as a John Barleycorn figure, having acquired a "mellowed silence" over the years. The poem has a simplistic but strong central argument: work with "fine intent" and hark to your gift, others may then learn, "Gleaning the unsaid off the palpable". There may be no easy, clear, instructions from the previous generations, but Heaney and Ireland itself may learn from what does survive, "the palpable". The pleasurable sentiment of the memories in the third and fourth stanzas is realised by the strength of detail: "Blue smoke straight up, old beds and ploughs in hedges". The beating of his father's stick echoes the concern with rhythm in 'A Constable Calls' and 'Casualty'. Here, nothing is "flushed" out, there is no clear statement. Whatever is to be said by his father is bound into the straw. *"The end of art is Peace"*. The quotation is from Coventry Patmore and Heaney told me that he found it quoted "somewhere in one of Yeats' earlier books". On one level it is a glib Victorian motto pinned to a frail device. But seeing the "spirit of the corn", becoming aware of the "burnished" warmth of its passing, enhances, intensifies the "frail device". The "love-knot of straw" is not thrown away; in a time which needs symbols of hope the "drawn snare" is at least a record of a harvest, it's "still warm".

The placing of 'The Harvest Bow' in this collection is important. I see it as plaiting together the strands of the whole collection. The "throw-away love-knot of straw" is a lasting embodiment of the sun, the life-force. The poem rests on that paradox and brings about its poetic resolution. What "does not rust"—there is a learned silence held in the twists of straw; each bend and knot both breaks and strengthens. Heaney is learning from the older man. 'In Memoriam Francis Ledwidge' follows this poem and the significance of the order is clear. Heaney is concerned with articulation; he's intrigued and excited by the possibilities of communication. The "golden loops" open out into visions: "I tell and finger it like braille,/Gleaning the unsaid from the palpable". It is Heaney's self-acknowledged task to knot these visions into language. The old Man's "fingers moved somnambulant", without conscious effort towards art; a skill that propels itself. The poet should, ideally, work in that way.

—Tony Curtis, *The Art of Seamus Heaney*, (Mid Glamorgan, U.K.: Poetry Wales Press, 1982 and Chester Springs, Pennsylvania, U.S.: Dufour Editions, Inc., 1985): pp. 118-19.

HENRY HART ON THE POET'S RELATIONSHIP WITH HIS FATHER

[Henry Hart teaches at the College of William and Mary. He is the author of books of poems as well as books on other writers, including *James Dickey: The Life & Lies of a Poet*. In this extract from his book, Hart shows the change in the poet's perception of his father from earlier poems. Now the poet is accepting and able to read his father's silences.]

Domestic covenants between father and son, which were collapsing in "Elegy," are mended in "The Harvest Bow." Here Heaney's father is a shield for his son, an icon the poet yearns to trust and revere, but the son's image reflected in the shield is the "lockjawed, mantrapped" one that Heaney delineated in "An Afterwards." For both father and son the shield represents the hard, silent, repressed mask that conceals and reveals the violence of their instinctual energies. Heaney's father is overtly brutal and appealingly mellow. He laps "the spurs on a lifetime of gamecocks" and whacks "the tips off weeds and bushes," yet in "mellowed silence" he weaves the beautiful harvest bows. The poem owes some of its pastoral quiet to

Keats's "Ode on a Grecian Urn" and "To Autumn" (Keats was Heaney's original poetic father). Heaney, however, is hardly as sanguine about art's ability to reconcile opposites as his early sponsor. Truth and beauty, like Heaney's contradictory need for both contemplative quiet and a bullhorn to speak against political atrocities, are at violent odds. The poem is as much a confession as an aesthetic treatise, as much a guilty, distrustful exploration of the tangled genealogical roots of Heaney's social quietism as an apology for them.

For Ned Corcoran, "Harvest Bow" can "be considered a revision of 'Digging'" (1986, 151). In addition, it harks back to "Boy Driving His Father to Confession," an uncollected poem written at about the same time (1965), in which a tender filial relationship is disturbed by the son's growing sense of disillusionment. Heaney recounts, "Four times [I] found chinks in the paternal mail / To find you lost like me, quite vulnerable." The chinks, in this case, reveal little of the man beneath the armor. So Heaney wonders, "What confession / Are you preparing? Do you tell sins as I would? / Does the same hectic rage in our one blood?" By the time he wrote "The Harvest Bow," father and son had been reconciled, paradoxically, by their mutual feelings of otherness. The bow twisted out of what Keats once called "the alien corn" is an emblem of their alien status, of their social unease and political disenchantment, their indifference to vocal protest against and active participation in current events. Both affirm the silent, peaceful art of making. But for both the silencing that necessitates art seems unduly repressive. Heaney groped "awkwardly to know his father" as a young man in "Confession." Now he offers "a knowable corona" that knots them together. To the question "Do you tell sins as I would?" he answers, "I tell and finger . . . [the bow] like braille, / Gleaning the unsaid off the palpable." His familiarity with his father's silences allows him to forge an understanding that approaches complete trust. His father no longer has to tell his son "what is going on / Under that thick grey skull," as Heaney rather indecorously put it in the earlier poem. Identifying with his otherness, his patriarchal silences, Heaney can now "read" his father's mind with all the assurance of a blind man reading braille.

Like Stephen Dedalus searching for real, artistic, and mythical fathers in *Ulysses*, what Heaney keeps finding at the end of his quests is himself. His father appears as his artistic shadow, not a cattle dealer worrying about the price of grain and farm equipment so much as a cultural totem, an exemplary artistic patriarch, an O'Riada or Lowell, who trusts the "gift and worked with fine intent" until his masterful "fingers moved somnambulant." From the talismanic harvest bow Heaney conjures up an image that implies that the child is father to the man.

—Henry Hart, *Seamus Heaney: Poet of Contrary Progressions*, (Syracuse: Syracuse University Press, 1992): pp. 128-29.

DANIEL TOBIN ON THE TRANSCENDENT MADE KNOWABLE

[Daniel Tobin has been Associate Professor of English at Carthage College in Wisconsin. He is the author of *Where the World Is Made,* a book of poetry. Here he explains the sacredness of the harvest bow, as well as its ability to perfectly balance both the masculine and feminine.]

In ["The Harvest Bow"], the "shown life" and the life of the poem become transparent to one another, and the poet's feminine and masculine modes achieve an equipoise. The poem is an overheard address to his father in which the ordinary bow is figured as a "knowable corona / A throwaway love-knot of straw." In other words, in its very actuality, its immanence, the bow harbors something of the marvelous and transcendent and, as such, the transcendent is made "knowable." Beyond that, the father has "implicated" his own silence into the bow, making it a symbol of continuity between father and son—a continuity between his "field work" and his son's poetry. Because, like his father, he is able to glean "the unsaid off the palpable," in his poem Heaney has made the bow an oracle that reveals the sacred, and gives speech to something silent. When the poet looks "into its golden loops," the past becomes present: he sees himself and his father walking together between the railway slopes, the father's stick "beating out of time." Indeed, since these artful loops "brighten and do not rust" they incarnate the sacred in their apparent timelessness and eternity.

In its quiet way this moment out of time within time reveals the source, the sacred center: "that original townland / Still tongue tied in the straw tied by your hand."

In a profound sense, then, "The Harvest Bow" fulfills Heaney's hope in "Digging." In that poem, he resolves to use his pen like his father's spade. Now, in "The Harvest Bow" his father plaits "a paradigm of art" which reveals a cosmic unity to which his son gives his own artistic assent:

> *The end of art is peace*
> Could be the motto of this frail device
> That I have pinned up on our deal dresser—
> Like a drawn snare
> Slipped lately by the spirit of the corn
> Yet burnished by its passage, and still warm. [*FW* 58]

The bow is linked to the feminine spirit of the corn, the Earth Mother in one of her more beneficent incarnations. That spirit dwells throughout the poem, holding male figures in an embrace as omnipresent as the center itself. The father's somnambulant fingers recall Heaney's vision of his poetry: "a kind of somnambulist encounter between masculine will and intelligence and feminine clusters of image and emotion" (P 34). "The Harvest Bow" balances both perfectly. Still, the wider intent of the poem is best clarified by the passage from W. B. Yeats's "Samhain, 1905," which Heaney uses as an epigraph to *Preoccupations*: "If we understand our own minds, and the things that are striving to utter themselves through our minds, we move others, not because we have understood or thought about those others, but because all life has the same root. Coventry Patmore has said, 'The end of art is peace,' and the following of art is little different from the following of religion in the intense preoccupation it demands" (P 14). The sacred import of "The Harvest Bow" could not be more apparent, though its motto understates Heaney's insight into the close resemblance of art and religion, an insight that divines them as having the "same root" as life. *The end of art is peace* "could be" the poem's motto, and that is what Heaney hopes it is. In a stunning image, the spirit of the corn slips through the drawn snare of art, as through the harvest bow. Peace, like repose, healing, and vision, is only promised. Its transfigurations are limited to what is knowable by their being made known through the poet's contemplative art, like the face of Louis O'Neill, "still knowable" though it blinds in the bomb flash. As Henry Hart rightly observed, to arrive at a pure peace would literally be the end of art, the end of the poet's work, an end that Heaney's poetry takes great pains to avoid." Again, what *Field Work* offers us as a volume is respite, not repose. Yet a hint of the sacred remains as a "burnishing" on the work of human hands. If the transcendent is present anywhere it is in those things that strive to utter themselves through us, though never fully rendered by our speech, but which remain traces whose force grows with the intensity of our concern.

—Daniel Tobin, *Passage to the Center: Imagination and the Sacred in the Poetry of Seamus Heaney* (Lexington: The University Press of Kentucky, 1999): pp. 168-69.

"Ugolino"

"Ugolino" is a translation of a section of Dante's *Inferno* and was published as the last poem in Heaney's *Field Work* in 1979. Heaney explained in a 1989 interview that he felt Dante gave "cosmic amplification" to Heaney's own contemporary world of Irish Catholicism. He described the attraction further in 1985 in the *Irish University Review*:

> What I first loved in the *Commedia* was the local intensity, the vehemence and fondness attaching to individual shades, the way personalities and values were emotionally soldered together, the strong strain of what has been called personal realism in the celebration of bonds of friendship and bonds of enmity.

Indeed, after *Field Work*, and especially in his next book, *Station Island*, Heaney would continue to translate other pieces of Dante and to use his themes. Heaney would translate into English, though, not Irish, signaling not a complete embracing of his heritage, nor a total rejection of British influence. Some sections of the "Ugolino" translation have been described as effectively modern, strong, and direct, others as having missed Dante's complexity and art.

The title *Field Work* brings to mind a focus on the rural, the rich land, the hopeful anticipation of a healthy crop. The poems that comprise it were being worked on by Heaney when he and his family retreated to a cottage in the Glanmore countryside, an experience of great growth and renewal. Yet while country life was described as familiar and comforting in earlier Heaney work, now in *Field Work* it is not so idyllic. While the countryside might offer refuge from political chaos, intertwined with it are guilt, abandonment, and betrayal. The theme of betrayal has appeared in other poems in *Field Work*, yet guilt, abandonment, and betrayal all reach their precipice in "Ugolino."

In this poem the narrator approaches Ugolino in the icy region of Dante's lowest depths of hell, just below the level of the betrayers of kinsmen and just above that of betrayers of friends, for Ugolino, who we learn was actually a count, was accused of betraying his country. The narrator finds him wrapped on top of another dead man, ravenously eating him "Like a famine victim at a loaf of bread." Yelling to get Ugolino's attention, the narrator asks "what hate" has pushed him to such carnal action. He asks for an explanation of what horror the partially eaten corpse must have done to Ugolino, so he can "report the truth and clear your name" to everyone alive in the world above.

Immediately, then, the narrator, who we come to see as representing the poet, sees himself as communicator to the world at large. Yet Ugolino tells him that his story already "Is surely common knowledge." The poet appears either out of touch with his people or of the belief that he needs to verify and expand on what the people know. More than likely, the latter is the case and he feels he must examine what is seen as "common" and explain why it actually is more than that. This is analogous to the situation of the poet, the Irish people, and the world at large, all of whom must attempt to understand the complexity of Ireland's violent chaos if it is ever to stop and if Ireland is ever to take a respected place among other countries. Curious here is the fact that the narrator poet readily assumes that the devourer is to be trusted, has been wronged, and needs to have his name cleared. There is no hesitation about taking sides, which Heaney refuses to do in most of his other work. Also, there is no hesitation about going further and saying he will stand up for what is right, a stance that has plagued Heaney for years as he grapples with the poet's role in public and during times of political chaos.

Before Ugolino relates his tale to the poet both his pain and anger tumble forth, as he explains that he aches just at the thought of retelling, and therefore reliving, the pain of his experience. At the same time, he hopes that the retelling will act as curses that grow upon his enemy. Pain and the inflicting of pain exist simultaneously, just as they do in Heaney's Ireland. The story focuses on describing Ugolino's time in jail. Little is said of the crime, except that Ugolino was accused of betraying his country, trusted his enemy Archbishop Roger when he should not have, and was thrown in jail.

The first thing that we learn is that the jail is now named Hunger, after Ugolino, showing that he has indeed achieved a mythical status. He relates a dream he had while suffering in jail, which turns out to be a type of premonition, wherein hunters chase after a father wolf and his sons, which are eventually tired out in the chase and then ripped apart by sharp teeth. When Ugolino awakes, it is to the sound of his own sons around him, crying for food. He stops the story at this point and says, in a parenthetical section, that at this point his listener should be most sympathetic. "If you are not crying, you are hardhearted," he says, and must be talking to the many readers of this poem, not just the poet, for the poet is before his eyes and Ugolino should be able to judge his sympathy. Ugolino's recognition of having a world of listeners gives the sense that this is a story that is momentous, or at least is so in the eyes of its teller.

That morning after the dream Ugolino and his sons hear the door being nailed shut. Ugolino knows it is the beginning of the end. The childlike innocence of his sons is before us in his description: "They cried and my little Anselm said, / 'What is wrong? Why are you staring, Daddy?'" They now have not been fed for two days, and again we are struck by the sons because of their loving capacity, for one suggests to the father that he eat them, that doing so "will greatly ease our pain." More days go by and then another son throws himself in front of his father, seemingly also offering him his body. Yet here we do not hear him offer his body, we only hear him say "'Why don't you help me, Father?'" Ugolino then tells us that "He died like that" and that within the next two days each of the other sons also dies. Since all is not clearly described, as in Dante's *Inferno,* so here also in the back of the reader's mind is the possibility that Ugolino killed his sons before they died of their own out of hunger. We are told that the father then died of starvation. Immediately upon finishing his story, Ugolino viciously clamps his teeth into the head of the archbishop, as if his revenge can never, literally, be satiated.

The poet narrator then berates Pisa, where this has taken place, for allowing Ugolino's innocent young sons to die. The unceasing repetitions of the "s" in the poet's chastising curses against Pisa reinforce its snakelike evil: "Pisa! Pisa, your sounds are like a hiss / Sizzling in our country's grassy language." Note the unexpected use of the word "language" here; yet it is most fitting for a poet to use, for in his mind a country's language composes so much of its self. The poet chastises, judges, and seeks revenge. "Since the neighbour states have been remiss / In your extermination . . . ," he says that he will wish Pisa's extermination by flood, alluding to Noah and

Biblical destruction. From these lines we realize that Pisa is not the only evil, but that the neighboring states are despicable as well. In the poet's mind, it seems to be only by their chance error that they have not already destroyed Pisa, asserting that they too are vehicles of rampant destruction.

Of course, this wish for the desecration of Pisa is yet another perpetuation of violence. For all of Pisa did not participate in the killing of these young boys. Ugolino is killed, his boys are killed, the Archbishop who did this is killed (we have not been told how), the neighboring factions kill, Pisa is cursed to be killed. Heaney uses the poem to decry the senselessness of continuing violence and revenge, both of which often involve innocent people and create chaos. His Irish people must stop their own violence. In the last two words of the poem, the poet calls it "my song." Even though most of the story has been told by Ugolino, he has put sound to the ideas and events, and if done well that sound will be absorbed and repeated by others.

"Ugolino"

[Tony Curtis has been Senior Lecturer in English at the Polytechnic of Wales. He has published and broadcast widely and his poetry has won a number of awards. His books include *How Poets Work* and his own books of poetry. In this selection, he sees Heaney's choice of "Ugolino" as his last poem in *Field Work* as a summation of the intense strife Ireland has suffered, as well as a warning of the intensity of future suffering if fighting is not stopped.]

It is significant that *Field Work* should end with the rendering of 'Ugolino' from Dante's *Inferno*.

> We had already left him. I walked the ice
> And saw two soldered in a frozen hole
> On top of other, one's skull capping the other's,
> Gnawing at him where the neck and head
> Are grafted to the sweet fruit of the brain,
> Like a famine victim at a loaf of bread.

It's a grim story and, unfortunately, is all too relevant to events in Ireland. One may see the Six Counties of Ulster perched on the map on the shoulders of Eire, under constant threat, so close to becoming "the severed head of Menalippus". The poet watches horrified as, mounted, his land eats off its own kind." They too "consort now underground"—the connections with the previous poem seem firm.

> Is there any story I can tell
> For you, in the world above, against him?
> If my tongue by then's not withered in my throat
> I will report the truth and clear your name.

That is the challenge to the writers in Ireland. They are charged with the task of reporting "the truth". In order to "clear the name" of their country they must recognise the complexity of the issues: the "tribal" divisions, the constant recourse of the British Army, the pressures of economics and the demands of nationalism. Running under all the public issues is the closed-circle of recriminations and reprisals, a centrifugal force generating chaos from the core of the Irish experience.

> . . . . for the sins
> of Ugolino, who betrayed your forts,
> Should never have been visited on his sons.

That is all too often the case in Ulster: you are born fatefully into one tribe or the other. The apocalyptic vision at the end of 'Ugolino' is a terrible prophecy of Ireland's fate if a solution is not found to the "monstrous rut" of the present strife.

Its effect as the closing image of *Field Work* compounds the urgency of the book's main theme. 'Oysters' opens the collection with a declaration of intent—the poet will "eat the day", consume the reality of violence in Ulster and work towards a vision that will match the depth of the tragedy around him. 'Triptych' points the way further towards a sense of political reality in Heaney's reaction to The Troubles, whilst the elegies that follow in the first part of the collection express the constant sense of loss which attends those who live in Ulster. Positive, human virtues are celebrated in the love poems of the 'Glanmore Sonnets' and the poems that follow continue that celebration.

—Tony Curtis, *The Art of Seamus Heaney* (Bridgend, Mid Glamorgan, U.K.: Poetry Wales Press, 1982; Chester Springs, Pennsylvania, U.S., 1985): pp. 123-24.

JOHN HILDEBIDLE ON SUFFERING IN "UGOLINO"

[John Hildebidle teaches literature at the Massachusetts Institute of Technology. He is a poet, critic, and fiction writer. His books include *Five Irish Writers: The Errand of Keeping Alive.* In the following selection, he points out Heaney's comparison of Ireland's situation and that of "Ugolino," where both the individual and innocents in the homeland suffer without any gain. Additionally, Hildebidle says Heaney's own attempts at escaping his Northern Ireland can never be successful, for there is no true peace in escape, only guilt over abandonment.] (. . .)

The landscape may still be full of familiars and relics, but what is clear even without the prior evidence of *North* is the degree to which escape is a necessary step. The sequence of memorial-poems to Colum McCartney ("The Strand at Lough Beg"), to Sean Armstrong ("A Postcard from North Antrim"), and to a nameless fisherman ("Casualty") emphasizes the murderous actuality of Heaney's former home; and worse yet the unpredictable intrusion of violence even into relatively unpolitical lives. One thing which distinguishes these poems from the attention paid to the contemporary Troubles in *North* is the relative clouding of sectarian lables. Heaney acknowledges his own politics, but only early on, in poems such as "The Toome Road" and "Triptych." Now the sects turn on themselves. The tribe which slays the fisherman is "ours"; bomber, victim, and elegist are all Catholic. In "Triptych," Heaney's sybil proclaims a dark fate for the whole of Ireland, including that part to which Heaney has "escaped": "Our island is full of comfortless noises."

Thus the nature and potential of Heaney's escape from the North is heavily qualified from the beginning; and the note of escape brings a countervailing sense of abandonment and betrayal, which culminates in Dante's story of Ugolino, with which Heaney closes the book. Ugolino's sin of betrayal places him very near the absolute bottom of hell, in the ninth circle. He suffers eternally just below the betrayers of kinsmen (a charge which Colum McCartney will level at Heaney himself in "Station Island"), just above the betrayers of friends (and Heaney, for all his affection for the dead fisherman, had, as he admits, "missed his funeral"), in the midst of those who have betrayed their nation.

Dante's curse falls not only on Ugolino but on his homeland; he calls down a purifying flood upon Pisa for including within its atrocity the deaths not only of the traitorous Ugolino but also of innocent children. The betrayal, in other words, is cruelly doubled: the person betrays the State, and the individual and often innocent human life is betrayed by the political forces within the State.

Heaney uses the poem in part as a charge against Ireland (and surely not only the North), which has shed so much blood to no apparent effect. But the focus of the poem is on Ugolino himself, the collaborator, and thus a man who tried, in a term Heaney applies to Francis Ledwidge, to achieve an "equilibrium," albeit one which proves, in the end, to be "useless." Ugolino's punishment is eternal cannibalism; he "lives" in hell "soldered" to his arch-rival Archbishop Roger (we might observe that all parties to this violence are Catholic), "gnawing him where the neck and head/Are grafted to the sweet fruit of the brain."

—John Hildebidle, "A Decade of Seamus Heaney's Poetry," *Massachusetts Review* 28, no. 3 (Autumn 1987): pp. 395-96.

MICHAEL PARKER ON EXPERIENCES OF PAIN

[Michael Parker has been Senior Lecturer in English at the Liverpool Institute of Higher Education. He is the author of *The Hurt World: Short Stories of the Troubles* and a reviewer of poetry, fiction, and drama. Here he points out Heaney's realization that he needs to understand others' suffering. The poem warns, too, that the future shows little hope if sons must suffer due to their fathers' sins, and if the people who are left have lost all spiritual awareness.]

Following perhaps the precedent set by Yeats in his middle and late volumes, Heaney has shaped the end of his fifth collection with a piece invoking memories of and comparisons with its earliest poems. The macabre fate endured by Anselm, Gaddo, Hugh and Brigata, the 'young/ And innocent' of 'Ugolino', has been anticipated by that of other *Field Work* victims, 'the murdered dead' of 'Triptych', 'A Postcard from North Antrim', 'The Strand at Lough Beg', 'Badgers', and 'Casualty', where the betrayal motif has surfaced already. The book closes as it opened focussing on the dramatic impact of political realities—on private living, the contrasting meals of 'Oysters' and 'Ugolino' emphasising the poet's acute consciousness of the gulf between his experience of suffering and that of others, and his determination to give others a voice, to 'report the truth'. The poet's guilty anxiety, enjoying the 'tang' of words and" the 'brine-stung/ Glut of privilege' in congenial, convivial company seems a far remove from Ugolino's terrible silence and grief and ghastly revenge, feasting on 'the sweet fruit' of his enemy's brain. 'Ugolino' takes us far from *Field Work's* lyric centre, a world away from the Owenesque 'underground' of 'In Memoriam: Francis Ledwidge', where reconciliation is almost thinkable. Despite its remote setting in one of the iciest recesses of Dante's Hell, one quickly adjusts to the surreal violence, the familiar, intractable territory. The two figures of the second and third line, locked into an all-consuming hatred, might easily be a Republican and a Loyalist paramilitary, an I.R.A. man and a Brit. If we pursue the analogy, as Heaney intends, Ulster becomes the 'nightmare tower', its innocent and guilty inhabitants plagued by moral famine, spiritual dearth. There, the 'future's veil' is 'rent', and children and young men can still be regarded as 'legitimate targets', despite the fact that the sins of fathers "Should never have been visited on his sons."

—Michael Parker, Seamus Heaney: *The Making of a Poet* (Iowa City: University of Iowa Press, 1993): pp. 176-77.

"Station Island"

Station Island is an actual part of Ireland that for nearly 1500 years has attracted religious pilgrims, with the current number of annual visitors estimated at 30,000. In southeastern County Donegal, it is where Saint Patrick did much of his missionary work and where, legend has it, he slew the great serpent that thereby made Ireland free of snakes. The Irish Catholic Church says Saint Patrick himself created the penances, such as walking barefoot on rocks, that pilgrims are to do on their trek.

The narrator of the "Station Island" poem, though, is not on a religious quest. He is a poet on his own pilgrimage of poetic enlightenment. In the poem (published in 1984 in a book with the same name), many of the described incidents and people have been a part of Heaney's own life, and we see an array of ghosts appear, provide advice, and vanish. In turn they provoke a range of responses, from wistfulness to apologies, fear, or confusion.

Section I does start with a religious tone. Sunday church bells are ringing, and the narrator as a young boy spies his neighbor working on his farm, with no intention of attending church services. The neighbor yells to the boy to stay away from the religious ones, yet the boy is sucked in, following their "drugged path." Not only will religion provide no solace for him, but it will ultimately be seen as a major factor in the violence in Ireland between the Catholics and the Protestants.

In Section II, the main character, William Carleton, embodies both Catholicism and Protestantism. Living in the early 1800s, Carleton grew up as a Catholic and was studying in the priesthood but then switched to the Protestant faith, writing works in favor of each at various times as well as writing novels. "Remember everything and keep your head," he advises in Section II. "We are earthworms of the earth, and all that / has gone through us is what will be our trace," he remarks, guiding Heaney toward the view of the poet as a vehicle of history.

In Section III the narrator is in church, yet remembers the loss of an infant sister as well as a lost dog. A missionary priest tells his tale in Section IV, home from a foreign land, sick, "rotted like a pear." He boldly questions what the narrator is doing "going through these motions" and disappears. A more positive meeting occurs in Section V, where Heaney is "refreshed" after having momentarily seen his old Latin teacher. Quickly, though, he is replaced by others along the path of pilgrimage, each providing positive commentary on the power of verse and the joy of learning from others. Yet this section ends with a twist, where a cynical trekker disparages Heaney for chasing him down. He eyes Heaney and remarks that some only come on the trip to meet women.

Section VI provides a respite from the resolute advisors. The narrator recalls his innocent youthful excitement over a beautiful girl, "Like a wish wished / And gone." Yet goodness cannot last, and so in Section VII he is shocked by a bloodied friend who had been killed in his home by Protestants. Here a request comes from the narrator: "'Forgive the way I have lived indifferent— / forgive my timid circumspect involvement,' / I surprised myself by saying . . . ." In Section VIII, though, he is not given the chance to make such a request. Here appears a second cousin, murdered by Prostestants as well. He condemns Heaney for not leaving his fellow poets upon learning of the incident and for not writing of it as he should have. ". . . You whitewashed ugliness . . . / and saccharined my death with morning dew," he lashes out. We are far away from the earlier, safe advisors. In response, Section IX is full of pain yet ends with the most hopeful thought: "Then I thought of the tribe whose dances never fail / For they keep dancing till they sight the deer."

Section X returns to the simple joys of morning, in this case seeing a relatively ordinary mug on a shelf. The poet cannot be deterred in his happiness, glorying in the "sun-filled door, / so absolutely light it could put out fire." A monk from his past comes to the poet in Section XI and, expanding on the previous section's revelry in simplicity, he advises that one never forget "the zenith and glimpsed jewels of any gift." But we return to a harshness in Section XII, where Heaney must listen to "the harangue and jeers / going on and on." This vehement new speaker is James Joyce, who tells the narrator that he must forget and that he has listened long enough. His words almost undermine the entire previous eleven sections that were full of remembrance and listening.

While it may make sense for the poet to hear that he should not flog himself too much for the past, as Joyce also advises, it seems it would be quite un-Heaneyesque to ever accept Joyce's further advice to not always do "the decent thing" for it does not always get you enough. But Joyce's role here must not be taken so seriously, anyway. For at the beginning of the section he is described almost as if he is blind, as looking for guidance himself, and, almost out of place because of its comedy, as hitting a litter basket. The poem closes with nature responding to Joyce with a cloudburst as well as some fuming and sizzling, alerting us that he not be taken as the definitive advisor. We are left feeling that the narrator's pilgrimage is still not completely resolved.

CRITICAL VIEWS ON

"Station Island"

BARBARA HARDY ON THE STRENGTHS AND WEAKNESSES OF
HEANEY'S CHARACTERIZATIONS

[Barbara Hardy has been Professor of English at Birkbeck
College, University of London, and Visiting Lecturer at a
number of universities. She has been a literary critic,
reviewer, and writer of poetry. She has written numerous
books on literature, including *Henry James: Later Novels*
and *Shakespeare's Storytellers*. Here she shows Heaney's
skills and struggles when recreating people, whether
relatives, acquaintances, authors, or literary characters.]

What one gets from Heaney's Dante, in the 'Station Island'
sequence, as from his Bog people, is a new structure for complex
experiences of childhood and adolescent recall, an ironic religious
sense, and a deep political unease. The new world is rich in images,
bright, witty, tender, and rueful, and in ways that are almost entirely
expressive of Heaney, not Dante. There is an occasional sense of
refreshed traditions, as when Kavanagh rebukes the pilgrim in wry
joking tones recalling how lazy Belacqua greets Dante, in purgatory,
and mocks his flagging energy. Dante seems to provide a form
which is conveniently occupied, rather than a meeting-place which
provokes fresh imaginative utterance.

But the drama of purgatorial withdrawal, contemplation, and
encounter with alternative selves, is skilfully contrived. The ghosts
are given splendid entrances and exits. Two worlds meet in the limbo
of reflection when "something came to life in the driving mirror",
and the novelist William Carleton crosses from one time to another
(II). A girl's image makes a surprise visit, "Where did she arrive
from?" (VI). A second cousin's mutilated ghost (recalling Colum
McCartney) "trembled like a heatwave and faded" (VII). The
disappearance of Joyce's spirit is veiled, as "the downpour loosed its
screens round his straight walk" (XII). These transitions are

unnerving in wit and ambiguity, imagined for modern and for other worlds. The conversation with ghosts is not Dantean, but a series of personal recollections, recriminations, and confessions. Heaney has no Virgil to guide and interpret, and must face his ghosts head-on, in powerfully particularised images and stories. (. . .)

The most willed and unimaginative sections of 'Station Island' seem to be those invoking other authors—Carleton, Kavanagh, and Joyce—where poetic passions are more sluggish than those in the pastoral and political poetry. Ancestors and peers are barely represented. Once again, the second term of a pairing is occupied rather than characterised. One has only to recall Auden's appreciative invocations of "black Tennyson", in *New Year Letter*, or the Freud, Pascal and Henry James of his character-poems, to see where Heaney's strength does not lie, or is not yet shown. Compared with these, let alone with Dante's bitter characterisations, his portraits are imaginary rather than imaginative. For anyone who does not know Carleton there is no vividness in section II. Joyce's voice is beautifully described as "eddying with the vowels of all rivers", and called "cunning, narcotic, mimic, definite" (XII), but the language and feeling spoken for him are not Joycean. His counselling words are definite, but not cunning, narcotic or mimic. There is another literary poem in the first section, 'The Birthplace', where Hardy is invoked in a similarly shadowy and obvious fashion, and where the strongest part of the poem, a reticent sexual anecdote, is much more interesting than anything about the birthplace, where some of the details don't even ring true. To see in a single bed "a dream of discipline" seems to neglect our knowledge of Hardy's tormented sexuality. Once more, Heaney calls to other images in order to have his say, not to make them strangely familiar or familiarly strange through meeting opposition and difference. This is domination, not discovery.

—Barbara Hardy, "Meeting the Myth: *Station Island*," *The Art of Seamus Heaney*, Tony Curtis, ed. (Bridgend, Mid Glamorgan, UK: Poetry Wales Press, 1985): pp. 153-54, 156-57.

DARCY O'BRIEN ON THE DISTURBANCE AT THE END OF
"STATION ISLAND"

[Darcy O'Brien has been Professor of English at the
University of Tulsa. He is the author of *The Conscience of
James Joyce* and *Patrick Kavanaugh* and has written books
on non-literary topics as well. Here he remarks on what he
sees as the narrator's and reader's distaste for the advice
from James Joyce at the end of the poem. Abrasive and
gnawing, one wonders if the narrator will follow it.]

In the twelfth and filial section (or station: the poem has all the
marks of a religious exercise, reading it or saying it analogous to the
act of making the pilgrimage to Lough Derg itself, though less
excruciating and shorter), the poet is helped ashore by a tall, blind
man carrying an ashplant, his hand "fish-cold and bony," who leads
him through a parking lot. The man's voice, "eddying with the
vowels of all rivers," is "like a prosecutor's or a singer's, / cunning,
narcotic, mimic, definite / as a steel nib's downstroke, quick and
clean" (92), and he strikes a litter basket with his stick and breaks
out suddenly into advice unlike any given before, impatiently
tendered to the younger, living Irish writer.

James Joyce advises Seamus Heaney not to be so earnest, to write
"for the joy of it," to "cultivate a work-lust," break free of piety and
the penitential, of all that binds him to the sectarian past:

> 'fill the element
> with signatures on your own frequency,
> echo soundings, searches, probes, allurements,
>
> elver-gleams in the dark of the whole sea.' (94)

Since the poet has just endured and shaped for poetry's and for
piety's sake a revisitation of the stations that have inspired his art up
to the middle of the journey of his life, made of these a haunted and
haunting meditation suffused with Dante, Sweeney, St. Patrick, and
St. John of the Cross, Joyce's impatience comes as a shock, impious,

a blast from Katharsis-Purgative, "indifferent as the herring-bone." "Let go, let fly, forget," Joyce urges Heaney. "You've listened long enough. Now strike your note" (93).

As Joyce's are the last words of the long poem, more or less, after which he strides off in the diurnal-nocturnal Gaelic downpour that sizzles the tarmac, he lingers, like a pebble in the shoe. We have to toss him out and begin the pilgrimage all over again to forget him. Then he's back again, irritating, disrupting like a cough or worse in church. One cannot help wondering whether Heaney intends to take Joyce's advice, to "let others wear the sackcloth and ashes," leave behind childhood, family, friends, as Joyce did in pursuit of his revolution of the word. When Heaney invokes Stephen Dedalus' April the thirteenth diary entry, calling it the Feast of the Holy Tundish, the collect of a new epiphany celebrating an Irish writer's claims on the English language—long a Heaney theme—Joyce sneers:

> 'Who cares,'
> he jeered, 'any more? The English language
> belongs to us. You are raking at dead fires,
>
> a waste of time for somebody your age.
> That subject people stuff is a cod's game,
> infantile, like your peasant pilgrimage.' (93)

It may be fruitful here to return momentarily, by way of puzzling out the effect of this Joycean outburst, this blast that reminds us that to the Irish, Joyce remains an abrasive iconoclast, even as to the Americans he seems to have become alternately the master technician and the purveyor of a message something like Gregory Peck's in *Gentleman's Agreement*, and as to the English he remains invisible and inaudible. [. . .]

—Darcy O'Brien, "Piety and Modernism: Seamus Heaney's 'Station Island,'"*James Joyce Quarterly* 26, no. 1 (Fall 1988): pp. 56-7.

MICHAEL MOLINO ON FACING THE "MASSACRE"

[Michael Molino teaches at Southern Illinois University, Carbondale. He is the author of a book on Seamus Heaney from which the following selection is taken, and he has written for many literary journals.]

In the course of "Station Island" a number of voices have been heard, various perspectives and experiences shown, and many contrasts rendered, all of which raises more questions that it answers. "Station Island" seems to say, like the granite chip in "Shelf Life," "*Come to me . . . / all you who labour and are burdened, I / will not not refresh you*" (SI 21). Like Chekhov, who let the horrors of Sakhalin prisoners and the indifferent bureaucracy of the prison officials speak for themselves without any guiding commentary or conclusive judgments, Heaney gives each voice and each perspective its due, most without judgment. (. . .)

The poet in section 1 of "Station Island," echoing the *Piers Plowman* poet, envisions a "field [that] was full / of half-remembered faces." The "Station Island" sequence certainly entails a varied procession of folk. The various victims the poet encounters reveal the many different faces of death: Agnes, the tragedy of youthful suffering and death; Strathearn, the terror of sudden violence and the loss of familial relations; Delaney, the valuable life truncated and the valuable relationship squandered; McCartney, the numbing inevitability of violence and suffering; and Hughes, the circular logic of martyrdom. Beyond the victims, three priest figures appear in the sequence: William Carleton in section 2, a failed priest; Terry Keenan in section 4, a doubting priest; and St. John of the Cross in section 11, a devout priest. At various points during the sections of "Station Island," religious rites and rituals occur—some performed in earnest faith, some in doubt, and others in mimicry. Even the speaker's perspective shifts throughout the sequence. Helen Vendler points out that "Heaney is sometimes (as with Joyce) the abashed apprentice, sometimes (as with his murdered cousin) the guilty survivor, sometimes the penitent turning on himself with hallucinatory self-laceration/" "Station Island," then, resembles "Singing School" in the sense that it too is a sequence of poems in which a number of different perspectives, points of view, experiences, and influences collectively act as a chorus in the poet's life. However, the poet of "Station Island" has not and does not plan to escape the massacre. He instead sees he must face the massacre.

In section 1, the poet announces himself a "fasted pilgrim, light-headed, leaving home / to face into my station" (SI 63). Far from the inner émigré of "Exposure," the poet of "Station Island" does face his station. No epiphany occurs at the end of "Station Island" that will place everything in perspective, make all things clear, unify and cohere all dissonance. Though the poet does refer to Joyce's words as a "new epiphany," they are really more an admonition or chastisement. Nonetheless, the realization that an object as simple as a household mug artistically translated might, to use the monk's words, "salvage everything," and that "What came to nothing could always be replenished" holds some promise for the future.

—Michael Molino, *Questioning Tradition, Language, and Myth: The Poetry of Seamus Heaney* (Washington, D.C.: The Catholic University of America Press, 1994): pp. 164-166.

SAMMYE CRAWFORD GREER ON THE TRANSCENDENT ARTISTIC CONSCIOUSNESS

[Sammye Crawford Greer had been Provost of Wittenberg University, Springfield, Ohio. He has written and spoken on Irish Studies. He is the a co-author of *Abolishing the Diplock Courts*. In the extract here, he describes Heaney's method of pairing opposing sonnets of "Station Island," to reinforce his belief that through ambiguity and confrontation comes enlightenment and balance.]

In "Station Island" the emotional trajectory of this process [of exploring the consciousness of the poet] is downward; ever more deeply and darkly into self-inculpation and artistic despair, following the path of the paradigmatic descent into the land of the dead, until the turn, in the middle of the ninth section, toward the transcendence that characterizes the final part of the sequence. This turn is reinforced by its location at the point of division between the octave and the sestet in the third of the five sonnets that compose section IX. At the beginning of the seventh poem, at the structural center of the sequence, the source of the memories informing this trajectory shifts from the poet's childhood to young adulthood and, concomitantly, from early religious and cultural influences on his growth as a poet to the pressures and burdens imposed by Ulster's sectarian strife on the artistic consciousness of the penitential adult. Memories of moments in his childhood, in the fourth part of the ninth poem and in the tenth poem, take the poet to the moment of revelation in poem X; hut this last part of the sequence is characterized by the growth of the poet's consciousness in the present and, in the last poem, by an anticipation of its future maturity. This curve of movement from the beginning to the end of the sequence is counterpointed by an interplay of reciprocal elements located in pairs of poems which stand in polar positions within the sequence (I–XII, II–XI, III–X, IV–IX, V–VIII, VI–VII). Thus, the progress of the sequence "through confusions and ambiguities toward a precarious balance" is informed by complementarities of varying and contradictory forces, and together these dynamic patterns culminate in the series of realizations that define the transcendent artistic consciousness. (. . .)

The source of the realizations in the last part of the sequence is the epiphany that the poet experiences in poem X as he recalls the mug that sat on the mantelpiece throughout his childhood. Contrasting with the darkness and the images of sectarian violence and death in the previous section, the morning sounds and light that provide the setting in section X endow the poet with a vision that is the opposite of his nightmare in poem IX. The revelatory nature of the memory that informs this poem is underscored by Heaney's allusions to the traditional setting of evocation: the brilliant light, the drifting smoke, and especially the "drumming" that suggests an incantatory ritual like the one in the last lines of the preceding poem: "the tribe whose dances never fail / For they keep dancing till they sight the deer" (*SP* 206). There comes to the poet's mind the one occasion when the mug was removed from its place on the mantle:

> when fit-up actors used it for a prop
> and I sat in the dark hall estranged from it
> as a couple vowed and called it their loving cup
>
> and held it in our gaze until the curtain
> jerked shut with an ordinary noise.
>   (*SP* 207)   (. . .)

In this epiphany the poet realizes the power of poetic utterance to hold "in our gaze" the loving cup that is also the earthenware mug: he realizes the power of poetry to endow the commonplace and the mundane with spiritual potential while faithfully representing the actual.

—Sammye Crawford Greer, "'Station Island' and the Poet's Progress," *Seamus Heaney: The Shaping Spirit*, Catharine Malloy and Phyllis Carey, eds. (Newark: University of Delaware Press, 1996): pp. 107, 108, 109.

HELEN VENDLER ON "STATION ISLAND" AS PRESENTING VARIED VOCATIONS

[Helen Vendler is Professor of English at Harvard University. She has written numerous books, among them *Poems, Poets & Story* and *The Art of Shakespeare's Sonnets*. In this selection from her book on Heaney, she calls the characters of "Station Island" the alter egos of the narrator, representing the array of vocations the narrator could have chosen.]

There are many ways to approach 'Station Island'—a poem full of persons, incidents and reflections. It has not been read as a collection of lives the poet might have led, but I have always seen its dramatis personae as a series of alter egos—men whose lives the poet, under other circumstances, might have found himself living. Within Heaney's family culture three choices of life might have seemed plausible ones for the eldest son: to inherit and maintain the farm; to become a priest; or to become a schoolmaster. Heaney begins by rejecting the first (see 'Digging') and (if we assume the usual Catholic suggestions to talented students) the second. He decides at first to train as a teacher. Yet the lives chosen by—or forced on— other men and writers of (especially Northern) Ireland remain as parallel existences in the poet's consciousness. Like the glossy young priest of IV or the monk of XI, Heaney could have found himself in religious life—at the missions or in Europe. Like Simon Sweeney (the tinker of childhood memory who erupts into section I), the poet is a 'Sabbath-breaker', but he turns away from Catholic observance out of intellectual conviction rather than outlawry. Though, like the nineteenth-century writer William Carleton of II, he leaves Catholicism, unlike Carleton he does not become a Protestant. Like the chemist William Strathearn (remembered by the poet as a member of his football team), killed by gunmen pretending to seek medicine for a sick child (VII), Heaney could have been caught in a sectarian ambush; like his archaeologist friend who died at thirty-two of heart disease (VIII), he might, given bad luck, have died early; like his cousin Colum McCartney (VIII), Heaney could have been the victim of an arbitrary sectarian killing. Like the hit-man and hunger-striker of IX (based on Francis Hughes of Bellaghy, whose family had known the Heaneys), the poet could have had he been brought up differently joined the many young men of his neighbourhood who became members of the IRA. Finally, he both does and does not choose 'exile'; like Joyce (XII), he leaves his birthplace, but unlike Joyce, he remains in Ireland.

I should add that although female presences in Heaney's life appear in two sections of 'Station Island' (his Aunt Agnes who died young in III, and the young girl with whom the poet 'played houses' in VI), these figures do not speak, do not become interlocutors of the poet as do the male figures in the poem. The female presences were—according to the poet in conversation—later additions to what first presented itself as an all-male poem. In the Ireland of Heaney's youth a young man's eyes were trained, in the search for his future, on male models.

—Helen Vendler, *Seamus Heaney* (Cambridge: Harvard University Press, 1998): pp. 92-4.

"The Haw Lantern"

We are challenged and examined in "The Haw Lantern" (first published in 1987 in a collection with the same name). The haw, a reddish fruit found on hawthorn trees or shrubs, has the strength and fortitude to still live and exude its redness in this poem, even though it is winter as the first stanza opens. Additionally, it has requests for people. But while the fruit has the vitality to be "burning out of season," such strong images do not persist in this first stanza. Instead, we are told that the fruit is only "a small light for small people," and that what it asks of them is relatively small as well. Specifically, it wants "no more from them" (again we have the downplaying language here) but to keep self-respect alive.

The last line in the stanza—"not having to blind them with illumination"—could mean that the people should not have to be made aware of the importance of keeping self-respect alive, that they should understand this on their own. It could also mean that the people should not have to be bombarded with illumination about anything else in life, implying either that self-respect is the most important issue or that they should already understand what else is important. Alternatively, and most pessimistically, perhaps this last line is saying that the people are too "small" to understand any other key insights at this moment.

A change takes place in the next stanza. Rather seamlessly we have become not listeners or observers of the action taking place in the poem but have become a part of the poem itself. In the first line of this second stanza, we are told: "But sometimes when your breath plumes in the frost . . . ." The poet is now using "your" and continues to use "your" and "you" throughout the rest of the poem. We, the readers, are now part of the "you," participating, just as the narrator, and possibly Heaney, now are participating as well. This first line is unassuming. How pleasant it is to hear the soft sounds of the word "plumes" and also to engage in the childlike pastime of observing your breath in the cold.

Yet relatively quickly the feeling is less easy. By the next line, the puffs of breath materialize into the Greek philosopher Diogenes, who is holding a lantern, which as the stanza progresses we realize is the haw from the first stanza and what gives the poem its title. From a bright fruit we now have a shining light that also may be capable of seeing inside men. The simple plant has extra powers. Diogenes believed that we must reject the pleasures of society and live a highly disciplined life. Here we are told that he is on a hunt for "one just man." The standards have become very staunch; there is no more smallness, no more single goal as there was in the first stanza. Instead "you end up scrutinized" and "you flinch" before the haw's "blood-prick" and its "pecked-at ripeness." The haw "scans you, then moves on," searching elsewhere. By the standards set here, at least as far as this scrutinizer in the poem can tell, you are not a just man.

Yet since the Diogenes in this poem is created from "your breath," he certainly is no impartial judge. He is a form of your own conscience, following your standards. Therefore, you have created your own test and still failed. Perhaps Heaney is commenting here not just on man's view of himself but on the poet's view of himself and his work. Since man and poetry are both works of art, they should approach the divine; their standards must be idealistic. At the same time, they must not lose hope in the face of such daunting goals, nor ever lower them. Similarly, when judgment takes place, it must be fair and thorough, whether imposed by one's self or an outside source.

"The Haw Lantern"

HELEN VENDLER ON HEANEY'S WIDENED GAZE

[Helen Vendler is Professor of English at Harvard University. She has written numerous books, among them *Poems, Poets & Story* and *The Art of Shakespeare's Sonnets*. In the following selection, she explains the evolution of the poet, and specifically Heaney's venturing into the "uneasy border of conscience" in "The Haw Lantern."]

There are two significant moments in the life of the lyric artist. The one I cannot take up here is the moment of the incorporation of the unbeautiful: that is a topic in itself. The other moment is the one when the gaze of the artist widens beyond the private concerns of the self. I want to turn to the evolution of the widened gaze as Seamus Heaney imagines it in three recent poems, published in *The Haw Lantern* (1987). There are many ways to the widened gaze, and Heaney's early poems suggest that one way is through consciousness of territorial borderlines that reflect conflict or difference. It is not until we perceive a group different from our own that we confront the choice of political inclusion or exclusion—that we even conceive of the possibility of a widened look at the world. Though Heaney's early poems had noticed the uneasy accommodations between Ulster Protestants and Ulster Catholics, it was in his volume *North* that he looked beyond his own province to map a whole arc of Northern countries linked by a common history of sectarian and political violence. In *The Haw Lantern* he takes the gaze yet further, from geography into allegory. Now the terrain is not Ireland, not "the North," but rather the unspecified "canton of expectation"; and, in another poem of this series, the frontier is not that of a nation or a territory, but rather the uneasy border of conscience (the unknown extension of an inner terrain).

The gaze can be widened, too, not simply by territorial difference, but in a second way—by the appearance, on the horizon of conscience, of an exemplary figure (one that Wallace Stevens would call "the impossible possible philosopher's man, / Who, in a million diamonds, sums us up"). This "major man" is a figure of ethical probity and accomplished human possibility. We have met him before in the poems of Seamus Heaney: in "Chekhov on Sakhalin" he was Anton Chekhov, visiting the penal colony on the island of Sakhalin in order to witness and write about penal conditions; in "Station Island" it was James Joyce. In the title poem of the new volume, the exemplary figure of ethical warning is the archetype of all such figures, the Greek philosopher Diogenes, searching with his lantern for one just man. (. . .)

In the poem "The Haw Lantern," Diogenes looks at, and through, the speaker and others with his lantern of a possible, or impossible, righteousness. One is expected, by Diogenes, to incorporate the stone or pit of fortitude as well as the blood of human frailty, to withstand being pecked-at as well as to continue ripening. This is perhaps the widest opening of the gaze, as the poem looks out to two limits—the extreme of human deficiency and the extreme of human perfectibility. Diogenes' scrutiny is a test no-one passes, but it continues to haunt the poet's mind.

Heaney's mode in "The Haw Lantern" is, surprisingly, that of the metaphysical emblem. His thorn-apple, his haw-lantern, is a cousin of Herbert's rose; "whose hue, angry and brave, / Bids the rash gazer wipe his eye." Unlike the allegorical parable, the metaphysical emblem as literary form is bright, visual, particular; it speaks of thorns, of the eye pricked by sensation, of the drop of blood exacted by insight. It marks the brilliant point where vision has both its sensual and its saving meaning; and consequently its rhetoric is often modest and self-obliterating, as it defers to the image seen in the eye's instantaneous grasp. The troubles in Ireland are generally interpreted in terms of Christian sectarianism; it seems to me significant that in invoking Diogenes, Heaney turns for authenticity to a pre-Christian standard of justice.

—Helen Vendler, "On Three Poems by Seamus Heaney," *Salmagundi* 80 (Fall 1988): pp. 66-7, 68-9.

FRANCES DIXON EXPLAINS THE TROUBLES OF AN EXAMINED LIFE

[Frances Dixon has been an editor for *The Critical Review*, the journal of the Department of English at Australian National University, and has written other work on Seamus Heaney. In the extract that follows, Dixon explains that for Heaney the difficulty of living an examined life is in the choices, which are not always the expected choices between good and evil.]

Throughout the volume, Heaney examines his life, and often sets the terms for his critics' "either . . . or" assessments of him. Images of judgment abound. In the title poem, "The Haw Lantern", the speaker envisages an external judge "scrutiniz[ing]" and "scan[ning]" him, and finally reaching a verdict. But that judge is not really external or objective: he is the product of the subject's very being—his breath on the frost ("haw"), his imagination:

> But sometimes when your breath plumes in the frost
> it takes the roaming shape of Diogenes
> with his lantern, seeking one just man . . .

In contrast with the way the central figure inhales meaning in "Alphabets", the speaker in "The Haw Lantern" breathes out an image of Diogenes, creates him out of his own need to be tested. This is no blank white page waiting to receive an impression, but pale "frost", filling with the "shape" that the speaker's *alter ego* takes in order to judge him. The "haw", the berry, its shape and brightness already suggestive of a lantern, lends itself to his predisposition for self-accusation, a need so deep that it "plumes" into the casually "roaming" figure of the cynic Diogenes who carried his lantern in broad daylight to emphasise the fruitlessness of his quest for "one just man". Heaney knows (as well as Diogenes does) that he is bound to fail the test he conjures up. Indeed there is no test he can impose on himself that would "clear" him, once and for all (and the poem does not imagine what such clearance might mean): if it were possible for anyone to face the ultimate test and not be found wanting, it would have to happen without the subject being

---

aware that a test was taking place—let alone deciding on the form the test would take. Heaney is concerned with the difficulties that self-consciousness creates for those who wish to live the examined life. In different ways, the poems in this volume are all thinking about how every choice of moral action in one direction means relinquishing the possibility for acting in another way; and the difficulty in "the examined life" is choosing, not between right and wrong, good and evil, but between different goods. It may seem that such a life is at odds with the berry's "bonded" integrity. But the people who suffer the anguish of self-division are as "bonded" as the "pith and stone" of the haw itself. Being obliged to choose between incommensurable goods is part of being alive, as is the difficulty of judging the choice made.

The idea that the examined life involves judgment recurs throughout the volume, but the concept of judgment itself is also examined and interrogated, particularly with regard to the question of whether it is possible to judge other people's lives, their combinations of choice and chance. Heaney wonders if there are any gold standards which might apply universally, or if circumstances alter cases so significantly that the very idea of judgment—with all its implications of an authoritarian imposition of power—might prove to be a subject to think about rather than a helpful way to think about a subject. And since Heaney is a poet, not a philosopher, he examines how his form of human enquiry might illuminate these questions.

—Frances Dixon, "The Examined Life: Heaney's *The Haw Lantern,*" *The Critical Review* 32 (1992): pp. 9-10.

DANIEL TOBIN ON MAN'S GROWTH

[Daniel Tobin has been Associate Professor of English at Carthage College in Wisconsin. He is the author of *Where the World Is Made,* a book of poetry. Here he writes about Heaney's view in "The Haw Lantern" that the tests one is confronted with lead to vision. With this vision, one is responsible not only to be a part of a collective but to foster individuation as well.]

[T]he poet remains faithful to the idea that art can transform the given material of life in ways that clarify human destiny. Central to that clarification is his sense of justice, in which the test of existence entails something more than words "babbled out." It leads to vision. This is the theme of "The Haw Lantern." In fact, the poem encompasses two very different standards of justice, one human and one transhuman. Over its course, the small berry is transformed from "a small light for small people" into a lantern that illuminates the soul. That transformation charts the growth in consciousness signalled by Diogenes, a figure who takes shape from human breath, from the *pneuma* or spirit. What Diogenes calls us to in Heaney's poem is an impossible standard of human perfectibility. The just man he seeks does not exist, or exists as an ideal. It is only natural, then, that the haw lantern embody a unity of opposites indicative of the highest levels of consciousness. The lantern is a metaphysical emblem incorporating the most rigorous spiritual discipline, attained only fleetingly by saints. No wonder Heaney flinches. But the haw lantern has political implications as well, for Heaney links its "double-vision" to Northern Ireland: Diogenes calls him beyond the limited consciousness of home. While on the one hand he believes the private consciousness grows "like a growth ring in the tree of community," he also believes "there is a second command besides the command to solidarity—and that is to individuate yourself, to become self-conscious, to liberate the consciousness from collective pieties." Diogenes is a figure, like Hermes, notably pre-Christian and unattached to Ulster, who calls the poet to fulfill this second command.

Yet the call to individuation is clearly meant to derive from a source outside the self, as well as outside the native boundaries. Though materializing from breath, Diogenes implies a justice that transcends self-judgment: "the wick of self-respect." So while "The Haw Lantern" offers "a true middle years vision of the function of poetry," Heaney himself clearly intends something more as well. As he remarked to Randy Brandes, "the function of poetry is to have a bigger blaze than that, but people should not expect more from themselves than adequacy. They should not confuse the action of poetry which is at its highest visionary action with the actuality of our lives, which at best are adequate to our smaller size. In 'The Haw

Lantern' poem, there's a sense of being tested and earning the right to proceed." The phrase recalls an expression that recurs in his poetry: rights of way. It derives from a farmer's indigenous rights to, or through, a tract of land, and appears prominently in "The Toome Road" as perhaps that poem's defining assumption. With "The Haw Lantern" we find Heaney once again reconsidering a previously held imaginative stance even as he follows his commitment to move on. (. . .)

Heaney does not assume the otherworld in his allegories, though the question of significance beyond history composes a key part of his journey. Redemption is kept alive in the question. Instead, the allegories of *The Haw Lantern* relate personal encounters to the historical and political realm. The question is not how to become a citizen of heaven but rather how to be a citizen of the earth, an earth in which human pieties take precedence over national and tribal ones. His allegories are stages to play out this question, stages on which the panorama of life and history and the panoramas of the soul illumine each other.

—Daniel Tobin, *Passage to the Center* (Lexington: The University Press of Kentucky, 1999): pp. 228-29.

WORKS BY

Seamus Heaney

Eleven Poems. 1965.

Death of a Naturalist. 1966.

A Lough Neagh Sequence. 1969.

Door into the Dark. 1969.

Boy Driving His Father to Confession. 1970.

Night Drive: Poems. 1970.

Land. 1971.

Servant Boy. 1971.

Wintering Out. 1972.

The Fire i' the Flint: Reflections on the Poetry of Gerard Manley Hopkins. 1975.

Stations. 1975.

North. 1975.

Bog Poems. 1975.

In Their Element. 1977.

After Summer. 1978.

Robert Lowell: A Memorial Address and Elegy. 1978.

Field Work. 1979.

Hedge School: Sonnets from Glanmore. 1979.

Selected Poems: 1965-1975. 1980. Republished as *Poems: 1965-1975.* 1980.

Preoccupations: Selected Prose, 1968-1978. 1980.

Sweeney Praises the Trees. 1981.

Sweeney Astray: A Version from the Irish. 1984. Revised edition, with photographs by Rachel Giese, published as *Sweeney's Flight,* 1992.

Station Island. 1984.

The Haw Lantern. 1987.

The Government of the Tongue: Selected Prose, 1978-1987. 1988.

The Place of Writing. 1989.

Advent Parish Programme. 1989.

Lenten Parish Programme: Renewal of Personal and Community Life through Prayer and Scripture. 1989.

New and Selected Poems, 1969-1987. 1990. Revised edition published as *Selected Poems, 1966-1987.* 1991.

Seeing Things: Poems. 1991.

The Cure at Troy: A Version of Sophocles' Philoctetes. 1991.

The Midnight Verdict. 1993.

The Redress of Poetry: Oxford Lectures. 1995.

Laments (by Jan Kochanowski, translated by Heaney with Stanislaw Baranczak).

The Spirit Level. 1996.

Crediting Poetry: The Nobel Lecture. 1996.

Opened Ground: Selected Poems, 1966-1996. 1998.

Beowulf: A New Verse Translation. 2000.

Electric Light. 2001.

Seamus Heaney

Allen, Michael, ed. *Seamus Heaney.* New York: St. Martin's, 1997.

Allison, Jonathan. "Acts of Union: Seamus Heaney's Trope of Sex and Marriage." *Eire-Ireland* 27 (Winter 1992): 106-21.

Andrews, Elmer. "The Gift and the Craft: An Approach to the Poetry of Seamus Heaney." *Twentieth Century Literature* 31 (Winter 1985).

———. *The Poetry of Seamus Heaney.* New York: St. Martin's Press, 1988.

———. *Seamus Heaney: A Collection of Critical Essays.* London: Macmillan, 1992.

Annwn, David. *Inhabited Voices: Myth and History in the Poetry of Geoffrey Hill, Seamus Heaney, and Geroge MacKay Brown.* Somerset: Brans Head. 1984.

Balakian, Peter. "Seamus Heaney's New Landscapes." *The Literary Review* 41, no. 4 (1988): 501-505.

Bedient, Calvin. "The Music of What Happens." *Parnassus* 8, no. 1 (Fall/Winter 1979): 108-22.

Bidwell, Bruce. "A Soft Grip on a Sick Place: The Bogland Poetry of Seamus Heaney." *Dublin Magazine* 10, no. 3 (1973/74): 86-90.

Bloom, Harold, ed. *Modern Critical Views: Seamus Heaney.* New York: Chelsea House, 1986.

Bloom, Harold. "The Voices of Kinship." *The Times Literary Supplement* (February 8, 1980): 137-38.

Brophy, J.D., and R.J. Porter, eds. *Contemporary Irish Literature.* Boston: Twayne, 1983.

Burris, Sidney. *The Poetry of Resistance: Seamus Heaney and the Pastoral Tradition* Athens: Ohio University Press, 1990.

Burt, S. "Seamus Heaney." *Poetry Review* 88, no. 4 (1999): 62-65.

Buttel, Robert. *Seamus Heaney.* Lewisburg: Bucknell University Press, 1975.

Carson, Ciaran. "Escaped from the Massacre?" *The Honest Ulsterman* 50 (Winter 1975): 183-86.

Cavanagh, Michael. "Walking into the Light: Dante and Seamus Heaney's Second Life." *South Carolina Review* 32, no. 1 (Fall 1999): 119-31.

Cookson, William, and Peter Dale, eds. Seamus Heaney Fiftieth Birthday Issue. *Agenda* 27, no. 1 (Spring 1989).

Corcoran, Neil. *Seamus Heaney.* London: Faber and Faber Limited, 1986.

Curtis, Tony. *The Art of Seamus Heaney.* Mid Glamorgan, U.K.: Poetry Wales Press, 1982 and Chester Springs, Pennsylvania, U.S.: Dufour Editions, Inc., 1985.

Dixon, Frances. "The Examined Life: Heaney's *The Haw Lantern.*" *The Critical Review* 32 (1992): 5-28.

Dunn, Douglas. *Two Decades of Irish Writing.* Manchester: Carcanet, 1975.

Durkan, Michael J. "Seamus Heaney: A Checklist for a Bibliography." *Irish University Review* 16, no. 1 (Spring 1986): 48-76.

Foster, John Wilson. *The Achievement of Seamus Heaney.* Dublin: The Lilliput Press, 1995.

———. "The Poetry of Seamus Heaney." *Critical Quarterly* 16 (Spring 1974): 35-48.

———. "Seamus Heaney's 'A Lough Neagh Sequence': Sources and Motifs." *Eire-Ireland* 12, no. 2 (Summer 1977): 138-142.

Foster, Thomas C. *Seamus Heaney.* Boston: Twayne Publishers, 1989.

Fumagalli, Maria Cristina. "'Station Island': Seamus Heaney's *Divina Comedia.*" *Irish University Review* 26, no. 1 (Spring-Summer 1996): 127-42.

Goldensohn, Barry. "The Recantation of Beauty." *Salmagundi* 80 (1988): 76-82.

Green, Carlanda. "The Feminine Principle in Seamus Heaney's Poetry." *Ariel* 14, no. 3 (1983): 191-201.

Hart, Henry. "History, Myth, and Apocalypse in Seamus Heaney's *North.*"*Contemporary Literature* 30, no. 3 (Fall 1989): 387-411.

———. Pastoral and Anti-Pastoral Attitudes in Seamus Heaney's Poetry." *Southern Review* 23, no. 3 (1987): 569-88.

———. *Seamus Heaney: Poet of Contrary Progressions.* Syracuse: Syracuse University Press, 1992.

———. "What Is Heaney Seeing in *Seeing Things?*" *Colby Quarterly* 30, no. 1 (March 1994): 33-42.

Haviaras, Stratis, ed. *Seamus Heaney: A Celebration.* Cambridge, Mass.: The President and Fellows of Harvard College, 1996.

Hildebidle, John. "A Decade of Seamus Heaney's Poetry." *Massachusetts Review* 28, no. 3 (Autumn 1987): 393-409.

Hill, Myrtle, ed., and Sarah Barber, ed. *Aspects of Irish Studies..* Belfast: The Queen's University of Belfast, 1990.

Jolly, Rosalind. "Transformations of Caliban and Ariel." *World Literature Written in English* 26, no. 2 (1986): 295-330.

Kearney, J.A. "Seamus Heaney, Poetry and the Irish Cause." *Theoria* 63 (1984): 37-53.

Kiely, Benedict. "A Raid into Dark Corners: The Poems of Seamus Heaney." *The Hollins Critic* 4, no. 4 (October 1970): 1-12.

King, P.R. *Nine Contemporary Poets.* London and New York: Methuen & Co., 1979.

Lafferty, James A. "Gifts from the Goddess: Heaney's Bog People." *Eire-Ireland* 17, no. 3 (1982): 127-36.

Lloyd, David. "Pap for the Dispossessed: Seamus Heaney and the Poetics of Identity." *Boundary 2* 13, nos. 2-3 (1985): 319-42.

———. "The Two Voices in Seamus Heaney's *North.*" *Ariel* 10, no. 6 (1979): 5-13.

Longley, Edna. *Poetry in the Wars.* Newcastle upon Tyne: Bloodaxe Books, 1986.

Mahony, Philip. "Seamus Heaney and the Violence in Northern Ireland." *Journal of Irish Literature* 11, no. 3 (September 1982): 20-30.

Malloy, Catharine, ed., and Phyllis Carey. *Seamus Heaney: The Shaping Spirit*, London: Associated University Presses, 1996.

McGuinn, Nicholas. *Seamus Heaney: A Student's Guide to the Selected Poems 1965-75,* Leeds: Arnold Wheaton, 1986.

McGuinness, Arthur E. "The Craft of Diction: Revision in Seamus Heaney's Poems." *Irish University Review* 9, no. 1 (1979): 62-91.

———. "Hoarder of Common Ground: Tradition and Ritual in Seamus Heaney's Poetry." *Boundary 2* 13, nos. 2-3 (1984/85): 319-42.

———. "Seamus Heaney: The Forging Pilgrim." *Essays in Literature* 18, no. 1 (Spring 1991): 46-67.

McLoughlin, Deborah. "'An Ear to the Line': Modes of Receptivity in Seamus Heaney's 'Glanmore Sonnets.'" *Papers on Language and Literature* 25, no. 2 (Spring 1989): 201-215.

Molino, Michael. "Heaney's 'Singing School': A Portrait of the Artist." *The Journal of Irish Literature* 16, no. 3 (September 1987): 12-17.

———. *Questioning Tradition, Language, and Myth: The Poetry of Seamus Heaney*. Washington, D.C.: The Catholic University of America Press, 1994.

Morrison, Blake. *Seamus Heaney*. London: Methuen, 1982.

Mullen, Fiona. "Seamus Heaney: The Poetry of Opinion." *Verse* 1 (1984): 15-22.

Murphy, Andrew. *Seamus Heaney*. Plymouth, UK: Northcote House, 1996.

O'Brien, Darcy. "Piety and Modernism: Seamus Heaney's 'Station Island.' *James Joyce Quarterly* 26, no. 1 (Fall 1988): 51-65.

O'Donoghue, Bernard. "Seamus Heaney." *Essays in Criticism* 50, no. 1 (2000): 88-96.

———. *Seamus Heaney and the Language of Poetry.* New York: Harvester Wheatsheaf, 1994.

Parini, Jay. "The Ground Possessed." *Southern Review* 16 (1980): 100-23.

Parker, David. "Between Two Worlds: Modes of Identification in Seamus Heaney's Autobiographies." *Critical Review* 48 (1999): 39, 46-60.

Parker, Michael. *Seamus Heaney: The Making of a Poet.* Iowa City: University of Iowa Press, 1993.

Pearson, Henry. "Seamus Heaney: A Bibliographical Checklist." *American Book Collector* 3, no. 2 (March-April 1982).

Quinlan, Kieran. "Forsaking the Norse Mythologies: Seamus Heaney's Conversion to Dante." *Studies in Medievalism* 2, no. 3 (1983): 19-28.

Sandy, Stephen. "*Seeing Things*: The Visionary Ardour of Seamus Heaney." *Salmagundi* 100 (Fall 1993): 207-225.

Schirmer, G. A. "Seamus Heaney: Salvation in Surrender." *Eire-Ireland* 15, no. 4 (Winter 1980): 139-46.

Sekine, Masaru. *Irish Writers and Society at Large.* Gerrards Cross: Colin Smythe, 1985; Totowa, N.J.: Barnes & Noble, 1985.

Shaw, Robert B. "Heaney's Purgatory." *Yale Review* 74 (July 1985): 581-87.

Stallworthy, Jon. "The Poet as Archaeologist: W. B. Yeats and Seamus Heaney." *Review of English Studies* 33 (1982): 158-74.

Tamplin, Ronald. *Seamus Heaney.* Milton Keynes: Open University Press, 1989.

Tobin, Daniel. *Passage to the Center: Imagination and the Sacred in the Poetry of Seamus Heaney.* Lexington: The University Press of Kentucky, 1999.

Vendler, Helen. "On Three Poems by Seamus Heaney." *Salmagundi* 80 (Fall 1988): 66-70.

Vendler, Helen. *Seamus Heaney.* Cambridge: Harvard University Press, 1998.

Williams, M.F. "Seamus Heaney's 'Exposure' and Virgil's *Aeneid*." *Classical Modern Literature* 19, no. 3 (Spring 1999): 243-56.

ACKNOWLEDGMENTS

Nine Contemporary Poets by P.R. King © 1979 by Methuen & Co. Ltd. Reprinted by Permission.

Seamus Heaney: Poet of Contrary Progressions by Henry Hart © 1991 by Syracuse University Press. Reprinted by Permission.

"'Inscribed in Sheets': Seamus Heaney's Scribal Matrix" by Rand Brandes © 1996 from *Seamus Heaney: The Shaping Spirit*, eds. Malloy and Carey by Associated University Presses. Reprinted by Permission.

"Violence and the Sacred in Seamus Heaney's *North*" by Charles O'Neill © 1996 from *Seamus Heaney: The Shaping Spirit*, eds. Malloy and Carey by Associated University Presses. Reprinted by Permission.

Poetry in the Wars by Edna Longley © 1986 by Bloodaxe Books. Reprinted by Permission.

"'Singing School': A Portrait of the Artist" by Michael R. Molino © 1987 from *The Journal of Irish Literature*, Vol. XVI, No. 3 by Proscenium. Reprinted by Permission.

"Representation in Modern Irish Poetry" by Eamonn Hughes © 1990 from *Aspects of Irish Studies*. Reprinted by Permission.

"Heaney and the Politics of the Classroom" by Lucy McDiarmid © 1995 from *Critical Essays on Seamus Heaney* by G.K. Hall & Co. Reprinted by Permission.

"A More Social Voice: Field Work" by Tony Curtis © 1985 from *The Art of Seamus Heaney* by Poetry Wales Press. Reprinted by Permission.

Passage to the Center: Imagination and the Sacred in the Poetry of Seamus Heaney by Daniel Tobin © 1999 by University Press of Kentucky. Reprinted by Permission.

Seamus Heaney by Neil Corcoran © 1986 by Faber & Faber. Reprinted by Permission.

"'An Ear to the Line': Modes of Receptivity in Seamus Heaney's 'Glanmore Sonnets'" by Deborah McLoughlin © 1989 from *Papers on Language & Literature*, Vol. 25, No. 2 by Southern Illinois University. Reprinted by Permission.

The Poetry of Resistance by Sidney Burris © 1990 by Ohio University Press. Reprinted by Permission.

"Seamus Heaney: The Forging Pilgrim" by Arthur McGuinness © 1991 from *Essays in Literature,* Vol. XVIII, No. 1 by Western Illinois University. Reprinted by Permission.

Parker, Michael. *Seamus Heaney: The Making of the Poet* by Michael Parker © 1993 by University of Iowa Press. Reprinted by Permission.

"A Decade of Seamus Heaney's Poetry" by John Hildebidle © 1987 from *The Massachusetts Review.* Reprinted by Permission.

"Meeting the Myth: 'Station Island'" by Barbara Hardy from *The Art of Seamus Heaney* © 1985 by Poetry Wales Press. Reprinted by Permission.

"Piety and Modernism: Seamus Heaney's 'Station Island,'" by Darcy O'Brien © 1988 from *James Joyce Quarterly* by The University of Tulsa. Reprinted by Permission.

"'Station Island' and the Poet's Progress" by Sammye Crawford Greer © 1996 from

Seamus Heaney: The Shaping Spirit, eds. Malloy and Carey by the Associated University Presses. Reprinted by Permission.

Seamus Heaney by Helen Vendler © 1998 by Harvard University Press. Reprinted by Permission.

"The Examined Life: Heaney's 'The Haw Lantern'" by Francis Dixon © 1992 from *The Critical Review*, No. 32 by Australian National University. Reprinted by Permission.

Passage to the Center: Imagination and the Sacred in the Poetry of Seamus Heaney by Daniel Tobin © 1999 by University Press of Kentucky. Reprinted by Permission.

INDEX OF
Themes and Ideas